I'm 25.
Now What?

GILBERTA THOMPSON

Published by:
Ellis & Ellis Consulting Group, LLC
954-439-0760

ISBN 13: 978-1546860891
ISBN 10: 1546860894

Printed in the United States of America.

TABLE OF CONTENTS

ACKNOWLEDGEMENTS

To my Heavenly Father, I bless You. Words will never describe how I feel about You. I thank You for the love you have shown toward me. I thank You for cleansing a wreck like me. From the moment, I let You in, my life has never been the same. You complete me in ways I never thought possible; without You I know this book would have never existed. Thank you for hearing my cries and sharing your wisdom with me. Thank you for meeting me every time I prayed and for not letting me give up, even when I wanted to. Thank you for trusting me to be used to write to your people.

To my husband Giovanni Thompson, thank you! You have been so supportive throughout this writing process. I have never met a man more understanding than you. Thank you for your words of encouragement and the laughter when I needed it the most. Thank you for being a listening ear, let me be real for a moment; when it comes to dealing with me, there is a lot of listening! Thank you for being my strength on days when I did not feel so strong; you are so amazing and I love you!

To my mother Stephanie Aritis, thank you. Every accomplishment or milestone I have received in the duration of my life, I call it OURS. You have been a driving force behind me when I needed it most. Thank you for your prayers, love, and support. I like to think, God knew exactly what He was doing when He gave me you. I love you more than words can ever describe.

To my sister Marjory Mauge, you are such a ray of sunshine. I thank you for allowing me to be a part of you and Patience's life. You have such a beautiful heart and I am so grateful to have you as my close confidant.

To my family and friends, I appreciate the love and support you have always given to me. You guys are so awesome and you mean more to me than you know. Thank you for always standing in my corner.

To my prayer partner, midwife, and sister, Dayvan-Rebecca Carey, do I really need to tell you what a gem you are? Thank you for the late night prayers and pep talks. Thank you for being the watchman that would always stand guard on my behalf. You are simply the best and I cannot wait for the entire world to see what God is about to do in your life.

To every person that wrote a testimony in this book. May God greatly enlarge your territory as you continue to advance His kingdom. Thank you for your love and support.

To my Kingdom family at Life Changers Ministries International, thank you for your obedience. Your ministry was the instrument used by God to change my life. Your prayers and support always came when I needed it the most.

My Apostle Valentino and Pastor Cleopatra Williams, you have affected my life in more ways than you can imagine. I thank God for the day you both said yes to Him.

To the readers of this book – Eyes have not seen, nor have ears heard, nor entered the hearts of man what God will do for you. Some of the most beautiful things are birthed through adversity. I pray that you will truly seek and hear the Lord as you read this book. I love each and every one of you and cannot wait to see what is next in your lives as you follow Christ.

INTRODUCTION

Here you are–you are at this point in your life where you want to know precisely what's next. You find yourself feeling stuck, lost, confused, or even spooling in circles. The more you think about "it", the more you become confused and you begin to question, "What is the point of this"? You want so badly to express these feelings to your friends and family but, let's face it; you know they will not get "it". Besides your life is your problem and nobody else's.

Don't be alarmed! The feelings that you are stuck, lost, confused or even spooling, in circles happens to the best of us. My friend, you are not alone. As a matter of fact, between the ages of 20-30, "It" is the point of a young adult's life commonly known as the Quarter-Life Crisis. Yes, you read that correctly, the Quarter-Life Crisis! But, what if there was a way that those feelings could go away? Imagine yourself receiving the answers and clarity to your questions, concerns, and doubts that have been challenging your life's purpose for days, weeks, months, and/or even years. What a feeling of relief that would bring to finally sleep in bed at night knowing your future holds purpose!

How do I know this is possible? Well, for years I to was caught in the Quarter-Life crisis. And, unfortunately it was longer than I needed at that. Not only was I trapped, but I noticed so many of my friends and family were entangled as well. Although I recognized the trend, I had no idea how to get out, particularly out of that feeling of being completely lost. I was troubled on every side because I could not help them, nor myself. I didn't receive breakthrough until I truly surrendered my life to Jesus Christ. It was then I was able to find peace and overcome this "crisis". As I overcame, small feats, the Holy Spirit would instruct me to share with others the process I went through and how I overcame having found purpose, peace, and freedom in Him. This book is not some crystal ball; it zooms into three core areas which, once mastered and applied, will change your life and end this Quarter-Life Crisis once and for all. These areas are perception, hindrances, and the ability to overcome.

Perception is your outlook on life. Often times, the way you react to a situation is a direct result of the way you think about that situation. Shifting your thoughts, ideas and beliefs from negative to positive could permit you to react in such a way that would improve the situation rather than deteriorate it. Hindrances, on the other hand, are external. You and I are fighting a real battle. Yes, you and I! Because there is an enemy, an opponent, who cowardly places hindrances in our way, we must identify such hindrances and tactics so that we are fortified to strategically fight–and win! This satanic fight is simply an effort to stop our progression towards our purpose. Your ability to overcome is wrapped up in Jesus Christ. God's love, faith, knowledge of who you are in Christ Jesus, and God driven purpose are critical tools that will propel you to overcome the Quarter-Life Crisis. You will find as you read each chapter of this book that my experiences along with the testimonies of other people share commonality, all overcame using a tried and proven solution that is Jesus.

As an avid Bible reader, I would be remiss if I did not include biblical references and stories. These references and stories serve an important purpose as they allow you to relate to several other biblical characters that experienced similar battles you are facing. Moreover, there are also several practical tips, principles, solutions, and exercises to ensure that you complete this book, equipped to overcome. It is my prayer and desire that this book changes your life and that you never be the same. As I wrote, I prayed and cried for your deliverance, freedom, purpose, and peace. I prayed that this book would reach the hands of those that needed it, therefore I recognize that it is not an accident you opened this book. This is not some random compilation of thoughts and manuscript, but it was birthed through prayer. These words come straight from the heart of God to yours. As you read this book, open your heart and let Jesus in. It is time for you to overcome, ONCE AND FOR ALL!

PART ONE

Perception

CHAPTER 1

The Quarter-Life Crisis

*So you are about 25 years old and you are experiencing "it".
You know, "it"! "It" is a topic that is virtually unknown. "It"
is not commonly talked about, however "it" is commonly experienced. Parents, family, and friends are observing your
life choices without recognizing "it'. Some may feel a bit worried, while others chalk it up to youthful bliss. They have no
idea of the confusion you feel when you think about the direction your life should be going. The way one day you feel
completely excited about the possibilities your life will bring
and the next day this same uncertainty paralyzes you with
fear. To be completely honest, you are not even sure what is
going on in your life. All you know is that you refuse to fail.
Problem is, the next step looks blurry. This blur makes failure begin to feel inevitable. I mean at this point, you have
completed high school or college, you are working some job,
paying bills, and you figure, **I'm 25, now what?** You say to
yourself, "this cannot be it for the rest of my life". You need
clarity, and you need it now!*

Well, this unfamiliar experience, which more than likely was not taught in any educational school system, is the Quarter-Life Crisis. Yes, the Quarter-Life Crisis. Just as the name suggests, around a quarter century of age (25 years old), many people experience a mental crisis. It is a period of feeling doubtful and not so patiently awaiting when your life will begin to make sense. The time where the word independent can feel so liberating and terrifying at the same time. Since everyone is different, the Quarter-Life Crisis does not always happen exactly at the age of 25, but it can happen between the ages of twenty to thirty. While it is a very real experience, many are oblivious to its existence and therefore have no idea how to deal with such a phase of life. Several persons will feel the symptoms without being able to identify the cause. Nonetheless, there are many other young people just like you experiencing this plateau and trying to figure it all out. Yes I know, it sure does not look like it on social media. Everyone's snapping selfies displaying their "perfect" lives. On the outside looking in, it appears there is no way anyone else is feeling the way you are feeling right now. Right? Wrong! The reality is that the Quarter-Life Crisis is affecting countless young people around the world–In. This. Moment.

Midlife Crisis vs. Quarter-Life Crisis

Many have heard of a midlife crisis but the quarter-life crisis and its validity raises question marks. These two life cycles are anticipated to happen approximately 25 years apart but are polar opposite. When I think of the midlife crisis, I see an older male (possibly bald) spontaneously purchasing a red sports vehicle speeding down a highway. He has worked hard his entire life and is now in need of some fun at any cost. The man knows himself however wishes to escape himself if only for a moment. He is not concerned about his life or its direction because he feels so bound to his responsibilities. In this midlife crisis, he is in need of some type of release and anything thrilling will do.

The Quarter-Life Crisis is the exact reverse. There is a young man that more than likely may not be able to just purchase a car spontaneously. He is trying to gain some momentum and discover his passions and who he is as an individual. This young man is running towards his true identity. The idea of responsibilities does not scare him, but rather his ultimate desire is to become more responsible and in control. There is no need for a thrill or disorganized thoughts but rather direction. However there is one word standing between him and his peace of mind. "**How**"?

Notice these two crises are distinctively different. One crisis signifies climbing up a hill to its peak and the other crisis signifies coming down a hill from its peak. Both the midlife or quarter life crises are not limited to any gender and can happen to anyone. So now that you know what the Quarter-Life Crisis is, how do you know if you are experiencing it? There are specific symptoms associated with the

Quarter-Life Crisis. These indicators fall under the categories of uncertainty, stagnation, and comparisons.

Uncertainty

One of the major signs you are in a Quarter-Life Crisis is the perception of uncertainty all around you. In other words, you are experiencing a lack of stability in numerous areas of your life. You may have had several jobs in the past few years. You may have also moved several times. Perhaps, you are having instability in relationships and friendships. Everything around you seems to be crumbling. No matter how hard you try, your future is just not shaping up and this is leading you into frustration. You are trying to figure out what you could have possibly done wrong but you cannot seem to pinpoint it. You think to yourself, "certainly all of this cannot be a coincidence!"

Your frustrations are now building up to discouragement because you begin to feel like maybe this is only a glimpse to the rest of your life. The fear begins to creep in because you are not certain if your life will ever shape up. The cousin of fear known as worry is now your frequent companion because you are desperately feeling the need to understand how everything will work out. This companion known as worry frequently visits you in the wee hours of the night and now you are losing sleep, sometimes even crying out of frustration.

Stagnation

Your uncertainty now breeds a sense of stagnation. You feel like you are in quick sand, unable to move, and sinking quickly. Your job is completely dissatisfying and the excitement has left. You long to be in a more fulfilling environment daily. The finances are not adding up either and no matter how many budgeting plans you make, the money is just not enough. Your friendships are not progressing or moving in the direction you want and you are questioning it. To sum it up in one statement, you feel stuck. As a matter of fact you do not just feel stuck because it appears that as you take one step forward, you take two steps backwards. One of the most common occurrences at the age of 25 is the feeling of lagging behind.

Comparison

The comparison game is up next. Not only is your life in a rut, but as you go on Facebook, Instagram, or Snapchat, it looks as if everyone's life is fresh out of a magazine. Even your favorite Hollywood movie pales in comparison to the perfection you are witnessing. Friends and families are getting married and having children while you are contemplating whether you can afford to eat take out. While you absolutely adore your friends and family, you are impatiently waiting for your turn to "shine" and be successful. Ok, let's just admit it! SECRETLY, you are a little jealous because let's face it, everyone wants to be happy. Your number one question to yourself is, "When will I be happy?"

I vividly remember all of these symptoms and feelings. Just like you, I experienced the Quarter-Life Crisis but at the time I did not recognize it. While I had no clue how to get out of the situation I was facing, I just knew I could not deal with those feelings much longer. The truth is, taking on the burden of trying to figure how life will work out is too heavy a load for any person. I just knew that if I decided to carry that weight any longer, I would break. At that point I had three options. I could go on trying to carry the burden until it broke me. I could act as if the burden does not exist and put on a facade. Or I could release the burden to someone who could actually carry it.

So I know you are dying to know, what did I decide and how did I do it? If and how did I come out of a place of worry to contentment? How in the world did I overcome the Quarter-Life Crisis? I wish I had some play book or some secret procedure, but instead my answer seems complicated but yet so simple. I called on Jesus! Throughout this entire book, He is the main character of this story. The testimonies found in these pages are just the voices of the supporting cast solidifying that there is truly liberation in Jesus.

The Effects of the Symptoms

Whether you want to admit it or not, the symptoms of the Quarter-Life Crisis have an effect on your daily life. Rather than living life to the fullest, you have entered a place of worry and doubt. The frequency that you over analyze and over think should be considered illegal in some cities. The main reason is because life has bought you to a place of trusting in your current situation rather than the One who is in control of all situations. You have misplaced your trust and now believe what is supposed to be temporary will actually be permanent. Rather than trusting the Lord, you are trusting yourself. You believe that the solution to your future can be found in yourself when really this could not be further from the truth. There are three realizations I need you to come to that is necessary to begin to peel back the layers and eventually get to the core of all of these symptoms.

You Are Not the Driver

Realize you are not the author and finisher of your life. Even before you were born, the Lord had a set design for your life. When you are the driver of a vehicle, then knowing the direction the car must go in is necessary. However when you are just the passenger, you can fall asleep and still make it to your destination on time and in one piece. You were not designed to worry. The Lord wants you to relinquish control and allow Him to steer your life. As He drives, you can find comfort in knowing your Driver will get you to your destination safe and sound.

> *Therefore I tell you, do not worry about your life, what you will eat or drink; or about your body, what you will wear. Is not life more than food, and the body more than clothes? Look at the birds of the air; they do not sow or reap or store away in barns, and yet your heavenly Father feeds them. Are you not much more valuable than they? Can any one of you by worrying add a single hour to your life?*
>
> *–Matthew 6:25-27 (NIV)*

Seasons Change

Our life goes through seasons. In other words, nothing ever stays the same. This Quarter-Life Crisis is just a season and these feelings will pass. The person that is in a Mid-life Crisis (the direct opposite of the Quarter-Life Crisis), once went through the Quarter-Life crisis. That person transitioned from one season to the next. Often times, a period of instability is really a period of restructure. Structure always comes before increase therefore before you can receive increase, your structure and foundation must be strong enough to facilitate the increase. As you leave one job, this leaves room for you to find another job that is more in alignment with the Lords plan for your life. As the restructuring is taking place in your career, the Lord can now increase your finances, passion, and overall peace. The prior job was not in vain because there were important lessons that you would have obtained that can assist in the next season of your life. It was all a part of the restructuring process. The same is true for relationships, ministries, and pretty much anything else. Always remember that seasons change.

> *To everything there is a season, and a time to every purpose under the heaven: A time to be born, and a time to die; a time to plant, and a time to pluck up that which is planted; A time to kill, and a time to heal; a time to break down, and a time to build up; A time to weep, and a time to laugh; a time to mourn, and a time to dance; A time to cast away stones, and a time to gather stones together; a time to embrace, and a time to refrain from embracing; A time to get, and a time to lose;*

*ime to keep, and a time to cast away; A time to rend,
d a time to sew; a time to keep silence, and a time to
:ak; A time to love, and a time to hate; a time of war,
and a time of peace.*

–Ecclesiastes 3: 1-8 (KJV)

Your Journey is Your Journey

Say this out loud, "I am exactly where I am meant to be in this moment of time." Repeat it, but this time say it louder! "I AM EXACTLY WHERE I AM MEANT TO BE IN THIS MOMENT OF TIME." Just because you felt you should have completed certain tasks or achieved certain goals by a certain time means that it was destined to be so. Everyone's path is unique. Your journey was designed for you and you alone. What you may be able to handle can absolutely destroy someone else and vice versa. This is why the comparison game is so dangerous. The marriage that brings one person so much happiness may be a train wreck to another. You may not last one full day in that persons shoes. While I absolutely love social media, we must be careful not to read too much into these platforms. Social media only shows a glimpse into the lives of its users. These glimpses are the best moments.

A smiling couple, a new born baby, college graduation, and good days on the job. No one ever posts the arguments between spouses, when the baby pooped all over himself, the struggle to complete college, and the days when the boss has made them feel taken for granted. The truth is, you may be comparing your reality to another "reality" that does not even exist. You are basically trying to achieve a façade of perfection which is unattainable. Your entire puzzle will fit together in the end. Steve Jobs said it best. "You can't connect the dots looking forward; you can only connect them looking backwards." Do not caught up and distracted by one dot. You will see the big picture when it is completed. While you may not always like it, embrace it. Your journey is your journey and completely tailor made for you! The moment I came to this revelation and realized that my life was not a race; the more I was able to kick back and truly enjoy the journey. Life is a journey and not a destination.

Before you were born, the God of the Angel Armies knew you. He knows every single day of your life. He knows what every moment of your life looks like. In other words, your destiny is written. This exact moment that exist, He knew it would exist. Quit pressuring yourself because everything in your life will fall into place the way it is meant to.

> Many are the plans in a person's heart, but it is the
> LORD's purpose that prevails.
> —*Proverbs 19:21(NIV)*

King David is a perfect illustration of what the Lord can do when anyone patiently trust His plans. While David was a young boy tending sheep, The Lord sent the prophet Samuel to anoint him as king. Can you imagine at such a young age already being sure of your destiny? Imagine while being perhaps a teenager, being told by a prophet of the Lord that you would be the next king? I know, kind of a big deal, right? No doubt, anyone that got this revelation would be super excited and ready to be crowned right away. However, before David could be king, he had to get through the journey. David also never rushed the process. Even while Saul was king and trying to kill David, David never lifted a finger to harm him. Instead David took it one day at a time, served, and waited on the Lords timing. Eventually, over a decade later, by the age of 30, David became king. Not just any king, but one of the greatest that ever lived. All throughout David's life, although the circumstances did not always look ideal, he was always where he was meant to be.

The Quarter-Life Crisis can be a trying time, but Thank God we are able to overcome through the Blood of Jesus!

Chapter 1 Checklist

☐   Recognize the Quarter-Life Crisis in your life

☐   Observe the difference between the Midlife Crisis and the Quarter-Life Crisis

☐   Identify the symptoms of the Quarter-Life Crisis

☐   Accept the 3 Realizations

CHAPTER 2

Expectations

Thinking Out Loud...

Oh to be young and free! To be filled with so many hopes and dreams. Not to mention the outpouring of imagination. I remember this youth vividly. I remember envisioning this entire world as mine for the taking. Naturally, I saw this whole planet as my canvas and that everything would fall into place exactly the way I imagined. I thought the moment I got out of high school, I would obtain this high paying job, save for a few years, build this dream home or apartment (whichever came first), marry my dream guy by the age of 25 (the latest), and ride off into the sunset. Never for a moment did I anticipate setbacks or trials or testing. After all, I had it ALL FIGURED OUT. My mom consistently warned me life would not be so simple. To which I thought, "Bless her heart, she does not know any better".

The truth is, I was so caught up in expectations, that I could not even fathom the slightest glimpse of reality no matter who it was coming from. After all, I had it all planned out. By the age of 25, my life would be so 'perfect'.

Expectations are a strong sense or belief that something will happen or come to pass. Whether we realize it or not, our expectation and actions are directly linked. It is easy to gain an understanding of a person's expectations in life without that person uttering a single word, simply because that person's actions will reveal it. Expectations are seeds that are planted and just like any seed, it will grow and bear fruit. A persons actions is simply a fruit of the seed of expectation.

There are four stages of growth from expectation to actions. These stages are as follows:

1. Expectations (psychological)
2. Preparation and Planning
3. Decision Making
4. Actions

When a woman is pregnant, we commonly use the term that she is expecting. Let's briefly take a look at this literal example. The seed of a child was implanted, so now this woman is **expecting (1)** a child. Due to this **expectation**, the mother begins to **plan and prepare (2)** for the child. Instantly, mentally she envisions a larger home, baby supplies, and other arrangements. **Preparation** is evident. As a result of extensive mental **planning**, this mother will be presented with different **decisions** and she has to enter the **decision making process (3)**. Rather than the **decision** of purchasing outfits for herself, she now has a **decision** to purchase an outfit for her child. Perhaps, she may have another **decision** to make as to whether or not she should eat healthy or unhealthy.

These are just a few of the various **decisions** that her expectation will bring. In the end, her **actions** will be rerouted. Her **actions** would not be the same as a person that is not expecting. Her actions will hinge from her expectations and ultimately, she will buy cribs, look for homes, and eat healthier. It all started from the seed of expectation.

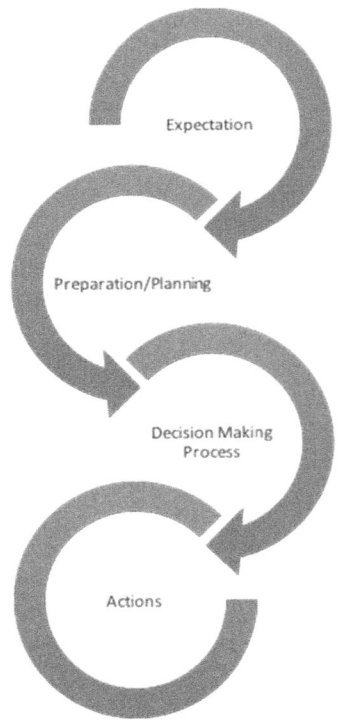

In the first stage of expectation, a seed is planted. The mother is expecting a child. The mother then enters the preparation and planning stage. She mentally reviews all of her choices so that she can plan. The next stage is the decision making process where the mother makes the best decision based on her seed of expectancy. The final stage is the action stage which is physical. The mother physically carries out what she feels is the best choice due to her expectations.

Filtering Seeds of Expectation

This same process commonly takes place daily in the lives of so many. You may be expecting to get married by 25, just like I did. Perhaps mentally you have begun preparing your wedding day in your head. You are now reviewing all of your options, however with a tainted perception. Actually, every single guy, whether it is at the grocery store, at church, or on social media, you begin to wonder if he is 'the one". Finally you meet a guy at the age of 24 and a half and because you have already planned your wedding, he must be the one. You completely forget about all the standards you have because your deadline is so close and your decisions are rushed because of self-imposed deadline and expectations. Eventually, your actions begin to manifest into fruit all because the wrong seeds of expectations were planted so many years ago.

This is just one of the many scenarios that show why it is so important to guard your heart. I could not express that enough. The whole truth is that seeds of expectation will take root in your heart, whether you want them to or not; however you get to determine which seeds will take root and which will not.

> Guard your heart above all else, for it determines the course of your life.
>
> –Proverbs 4:23(NLT)

Perhaps you may be allowing everything around you into your heart without filtering it and as a result, the wrong expectations are taking root. This may include watching soap operas that fantasize marriage, listening to music that glorifies houses, cars, luxury, and being young and rich. It could be you are watching the lives of those around you and allowing comparisons to breed expectations. You see that everyone else is having kids and seem to be progressing, so you transfer expectations from the life of someone else and allow it to take root into your life.

Not only should you be careful of self-imposed expectations, but you must also be careful not to transfer the expectations from the lives of others into your life. So often I have seen persons that are talented, smart, and so filled with potential allow the expectations of those around them to dictate their life. Perhaps it may be a parent saying you may not amount to anything. Those words and expectation of that parent has been rooted in your heart from childhood. You find that no matter what you do in life, whenever any type of perceived failure occurs, you trace it back to those same words. It may have been an ex-boyfriend that said no one would ever love you and now you begin to feel unloved because that seed has also been planted. You find yourself acting unworthy of love in future relationships. Oh, be careful little hearts, what you let in.

The whole purpose of a filter is to rid anything that comes through that filter of impurities and leave behind only pure substances. In other words the filter is separating two components, leaving that which does not belong behind. Are you filtering your heart and guarding it from impurities? If not, now would be a perfect time to start so that the wrong contaminated expectations, whether by you or others, will not be planted and produce fruit into your life.

Expectations in the form of dreams, plans, and goals are all beautiful. Believe me, I had many. But these goals were missing one critical ingredient. As a matter of fact, it was the greatest or secret ingredient. I did not at any point include the Lords plans or desires for my life. I thought I had it all figured out forgetting that the Creator of the Universe may have taken another route with me. To be frank, I would not even give Him a chance to input His expectations for my life because I was simply afraid. Truly, I was petrified that His plans would differ from my plans. Totally selfish, I know. But I wanted what I wanted. I thought suppose He told me to get married at 30. Oh the horror! Even worst, suppose He told me to listen to my mother. An even bigger horror. The truth is, I was just plain old stubborn.

The error with this way of thinking is that our entire existence is centered around Jesus Christ, not the other way around. The Lord created each and every one of us with an intended purpose in mind. As the Creator of this purpose, He and Him alone holds the map. Not you, your parents, your spouse or anyone else. As the holder of this map, the Lord directs your path. He tells you when to turn left, right, or go straight. You may wonder, how will I know when it is the Lord directing my path? The answer may seem complicated but it is actually quite simple.

As a child, even before completely understanding, somehow we all knew when we were doing something right or wrong. Even as toddlers, we would somehow just know. No one had to say this is wrong, however the feeling of 'wrongness' just existed whenever certain acts occurred. Now take a minute, and think of other times this exact feeling of 'wrongness' may have occurred. The truth is it never went away. This feeling is carried straight over into adulthood. In this similar way, the Lord directs our paths as we seek Him. He will give you a "feeling" when you are going left instead of right. You will also know when you are going down the right path. I often hear persons say, I had a feeling this was going to happen. Well it's not just a feeling. It is actually the Lord guiding you, convicting you, and tugging at your heart, through the Holy Spirit, once you have accepted Him. Somehow, some way, you will just know you are making the right decision and when you look back, it will be complete confirmation that it was indeed the Lord guiding you. Do not be discouraged if you do not have full understanding of all the decisions the Lord is asking you to make because it is God's plan not yours. You will not always fully understand it. Not having all the answers will sometimes be a hard pill to swallow but once you follow His instructions, it will all make sense in the end.

Now expectations are not all bad. It is just the wrong expectations that can be harmful. There is a big difference between Godly expectations and humanly expectations. Godly expectations are those expectations which are in alignment or birthed from God's perfect will for your life. The Lord has given many promises to His children, therefore to be in complete expectancy of these promises, provided you are His child, is completely normal. So if the Lord says, by His stripes you are healed, which is His will, it is perfectly normal to expect healing. Perhaps the Lord promised you a house or marriage before 25, then it is perfectly fine to expect based on the promises of God. As a matter of fact, as an individual grows into a relationship with Christ, it is beneficial that your will conforms to God's will or in other words, expect God's will. You should never try to conform Gods will to your will. Here is a biblical example of one king and how both types of expectations (human and Godly expectations) provided different outcomes for two different wars.

Human Expectations

King Jehoshaphat was a king of Judah that loved God. He followed God in all his ways, however he made an alliance with King Ahab, who was the King of Israel. Unlike Jehoshaphat, Ahab was an evil man in the sight of God. Ahab wanted to attack Ramoth (another city) and desired to use his alliance with Jehoshaphat to do so. Ahab's expectation was to attack this country and win the war. Being the man of God that Jehoshaphat was, he wanted to seek Godly counsel before acting.

So Ahab bought 400 prophets in for counsel. All of the prophets concluded that the war would be won by the kings. Still not satisfied, King Jehoshaphat asked if there were not any other prophets that he could hear from. King Ahab then sent for Micaiah, who then came in with a contrary prophecy. Despite being pressured by the other prophets to unanimously state that the kings would win the war, he said exactly what God said. Independently, Micaiah shared Gods word and said that the war will be lost. Not just any defeat, but a horrible defeat. He even prophesied that King Ahab would die. Despite this word, the kings still decided to go to war.

In this story, we see that King Ahab had his humanly expectations. He anticipated that he would win the war. So much that he ignored the word of Gods very own true prophet. Instead, King Ahab wanted Gods word to conform to his expectations which is why he found it so easy to believe the 400 prophets that were lying. His actions of going into war despite what God said and knew would happen was all because of carnal expectations. His expectations were reliant on his limited knowledge. There are consequences for allowing human expectations to lead your life and in this case, death was the consequence for King Ahab.

How many times have you seen persons make selfish decisions and allow human expectations to lead? Even I have been guilty on numerous occasions. Like, you know the Lord has already spoken and said that particular relationship is unhealthy. Possibly He has told you that it is time to leave that job. Perhaps that feeling of 'wrongness' is haunting you right now over a major decision, but because you are relying on your human expectation that everything will work out, you completely disregard Gods word and go on with everyday living. No matter the situation, know that Gods word does not lie. Just as King Ahab faced consequences for his disobedience, there are also consequences attached to your disobedience. It is always better to be obedient than to experience sacrifice. The good news is it is never too late to repent and walk in obedience.

Godly Expectations

Later on in Jehoshaphat's life, three countries joined forces to come against Judah. This time, Jehoshaphat sought the Lord directly. King Jehoshaphat ordered a nationwide fast. Persons from all over Judah came to pray. In the midst of this assembly, the Spirit of the Lord came upon a man by the name of Jahaziel. He spoke up and declared that the Lord said He would fight this war on behalf of Judah. Jahaziel also further stated that Judah must go out and meet their opposition, however they would not have to lift so much as a finger. Jehoshaphat and the nation Judah worshipped the Lord. Judah was obedient and headed towards the battle field singing praises to God. In the end, all of Judah's enemies got confused and ended up killing each other. The war was won without Judah even having to fight.

This is a second instance of war by the same king, however he relied on God's word before he formed expectations. Jehoshaphat did not just automatically expect defeat since he was so largely outnumbered. He decided not to allow human expectations to cloud his judgement this time. His expectations were built based on Gods plan, and it showed in Judah's actions and obedience. When you apply these same principles in your daily lives, the Lord ends up fighting your battles for you. You start to feel joyful instead of depressed without even understanding why. You begin to develop a hopeful outlook on life, rather than feeling purposeless. Rebellious children become obedient without you having to say a word. The Lord begins to fight!

It is absolutely dangerous to place your limited goals, perceptions, and yes even age limits on God. Anything that is placed before God can be considered an idol; this can even include your expectations. Expectations become an idol when you prefer your expectations rather than God. Some may expect to be married by a certain time so these persons end up spending time on dating sites and match making rather than spending time with God. Others may expect to buy a home before a certain age so these persons end up forcing loans, rather than waiting for Gods set time and provision.

Another may expect to have children by a certain age, so this person partakes in risky behavior rather than awaiting God. Once your expectations take the place of trusting God, it instantly becomes your idol. In making expectations an idol, this only leaves open doorways for setbacks, disappointments, depression, and impatience. The Lord is aware you are 25 or older. He is also aware of His plan and where He wants to take you.

> For I know the plans I have for you," declares the LORD, "plans to prosper you and not to harm you, plans to give you hope and a future.
> –Jeremiah 29:11 (NIV)

Since the Lord sees the entire picture for your life. Not just the present. The Lord will give you the wisdom to make decisions for today that will prosper you tomorrow. Let's use an example of a person driving a vehicle straight into a storm. If the person is unaware that the storm is ahead, that person will make decisions as if there is no storm ahead. Some of these decisions will even make damages caused by the storm more severe due to lack of preparation. But if there was a person ahead of the storm able to contact that individual and let them know how to prepare for the storm and avoid it if possible, then the person driving the car would be better off down the road. Well the Lord is that all powerful God always ahead of every situation or storm life can possible throw. He is able to direct your path, but only if you rely on Him rather than your limited expectations. If the very hairs on your head are numbered, do you not think the Lord is concerned with every single aspect of your life?

> *"Indeed the very hairs of your head are all numbered. Don't be afraid; you are worth many sparrows"*
>
> *–Luke 12:7 (NIV)*

Constantly reminding The Lord of what you want and expect Him to do will not make the journey any more pleasant. Rather, trust in Him, rest in Him, and have peace in Him.

Here comes the fun part! On the next page, make a list of every expectation in your life that you desire God to fulfill. I am not speaking of promises the Lord has made to you, but expectations that were planted by self or others rather than God.

Spend time praying and seeking God to reveal if these expectations are in alignment with His perfect will for your life. Be patient, the answer will not come right away but as you continue to ask the Lord, He will reveal it to you. You will know the answer based on your peace. If there is anything on this list that you do not feel peaceful about, you will know it is not God. Simply ask the Lord to help you remove these expectations from your heart and to truly release them. Make a decision and refuse to be ruled by expectations but rather by Gods plan. Throw away idol expectations and live in total submission to His will.

Testimony Corner

Before I came to know Christ, I must admit, I really did not have any expectations in regards to my life. I didn't hope, wish or plan for anything to happen in my future. I simply took life as it came from day to day. I figured thinking this way would save me from unnecessary disappointments when my life didn't unfold exactly the way that I had projected it to. When, on the contrary, having this mentality only left me feeling void, as I merely went through life existing and not truly living to my maximum potential. Then at age 21, I dedicated my life to the Lord. As I learned to pray, His presence began to fill the empty places in my life and I became filled with a spirit of expectancy. Yes, for the first time in life I started to hope that my life could be so much more gratifying. Can I say that from here on out I thought my life would be perfect, because after all I was now a Christian.

I recall one day when I felt impregnated with the excitement of planning for my future. I pulled out all the show stoppers that day. I went to multiple stores and purchased journals, daily planners, oversized calendars, sticky posts with highlighters and loads of colorful inked pens. I started writing down dozens of ambitions that I desired to accomplish by the time I was 25 years old. That's right

I had written a two-page (okay three-page) master checklist of the things that I MUST accomplish over the next 4 years. It was my utmost determination that every single deadline and goal be met. I told myself that by that time, I would be married to a 6 foot 2 inches tall, muscular built, well- established, handsome man of God. I would be living in my own immaculate home with a white picket fence, luscious garden and an elegant welcome mat at the front door. And of course, my ultimate aspiration at that time was that I would graduate from college with my baccalaureate of Science degree in Nursing, as the class valedictorian. I couldn't imagine it any other way. Better yet, I did not allow myself to perceive that life would happen and perhaps that's where my issue came in.

While nothing was wrong with forecasting a bright future, and having great expectation, I had a tunnel vision that life was supposed to turn out exactly the way that I had anticipated. I didn't expect that anything could now go wrong. Imagine my unpleasant surprise when my 25th birthday found me unemployed, having to seek welfare assistance from the Social Services Department. I was broken hearted, ever so single, and secretly battling with depression. All while still living at home with my mother. To make matters worse, I had been suspended from my scholarship and set back a year in my studies due to failing a major nursing course. Shamefully, it was now my eighth year in college. It was far beyond how I had predicted my life would have been at that point. I kept pondering on several things that constantly weighed on my heart: 1) Where did I go wrong? 2)Were my standards too high? 3)Why was my life taking so long to get in order? 4) Would it ever be my time to have a happy ending? I didn't comprehend why my life was taking a turn for the worst now that I had gotten on the right track by taking the step to become a Christian. I thought that it would have been smooth sailing. I never thought I would get caught up in the winds of a chaotic life-storm. Some days I got to the point where I felt as though perhaps I didn't deserve success, love, or happiness. I began to become comfortable with simply accepting the hand that life had dealt me. I became numb to failure and disappointment. In fact, the only thing I began to expect was that every dream that I had for my life would self-destruct in front of my eyes. I wanted to simply throw my dreams to the winds and give up on hope. I literally became afraid of writing goals down, much less praying for my future, because it appeared as if every good thing I had intended to happen would go haywire instead.

There were moments when I thought that I was on the brink of entirely giving up. Yet, somehow when my mind and my body would be exhausted from catching the curve balls that life continuously threw at me, my heart would still grab a hold of whatever residue of hope that remained. I wondered how my heart could still dare to anticipate that a breakthrough was coming my way, even when displeasures stared me directly in the face. Then one day while reading my bible the answer came to me. Romans 8:28 (KJV) says "and we know that all things work together for good to them that love God, to them who are called according to His purpose". I could not begin to explain how my mindset literally changed overnight. I now understood that being a Christian did not exempt me from having unplanned and undesired circumstances from happening in my life. I also realized that fearing for my future had paralyzed my ability to hope. Faith had to become my antidote to fear. So, I began to believe and expect that even when situations went contrary to how I had planned, every single thing would work out for the better because my life had a purpose larger than my dreams.

As my outlook on life became optimistic, my level of expectancy increased. Instantaneously, life began to turn around and doors of opportunities opened for me. In the year that I was setback from completing my degree I was elected President of the Student Nurses Association. This allowed numerous opportunities such as being invited as a motivational speaker at numerous events and meeting various influential people. I was humbled and amazed to see how, in one short year, my pitfall became my platform to inspire others to dream and push beyond their feelings to achieve their goals. Although I didn't have the opportunity to graduate as valedictorian, I was given the opportunity to deliver a heart-felt presentation to the graduates during our Nursing Pinning Ceremony. The thing is, it took me nearly 10 years (yes, almost a decade) to complete my undergraduate degree, but it was worth the wait and the ceremony was even better than I had ever imagined.

What I thought was the close to one chapter in my life was actually the prologue to pages that had just begun to unfold, displaying a new beginning in my life. Swiftly, in less than 6 months of being hired as a Registered Nurse, I was selected to be a part of a training course that would permit me to work in a new State-of- the-art facility that took nearly 10 years to complete and open. Was this a coincidence? Perhaps... but I choose to call it fate. See on the contrary, when it may have appeared as though I was behind schedule to receive my blessing in regards to my career, I was right on time! Things that I hadn't even conceptualized began to happen. To my surprise, just after one year of working as a junior nurse, my supervisor selected me to develop a nursing-led program managing patients with Developmental Disabilities in the same brand new facility. My supervisor stated that I was chosen because of my passion, creativity, dedication, and leadership ability. I was baffled that they selected me when so many others with more years of experience could fit the profile. I couldn't believe it, but I received it! Although it wasn't technically a promotion, it was a tremendous advancement in my career, as I was given the leeway to be my own boss. I could not have imagined the acceleration that would have taken place in the first year of my nursing career. This was nowhere in my planning. I had never even come close to putting this on my dream board. No, instead this blew my mind.

It's funny I now understand that my expectations were not too big, but rather too small. Things began working out even better than I had imagined, the more I trusted in God's plan for my life and not simply my own. Yes, I still plan a head for my future with great anticipation, but I have also learnt to take the limitations off my level of expectation. Ephesians 3:20 is a scripture that kindles my spirit of expectancy. It states, "Now unto Him that is able to do exceeding, abundant, above all we can ask, think, or even imagine; according to the power that worketh in us". Every time I thought that things could not possibly get any better, it did. Every time I turned around there was a "but wait there's more" kind of blessing. You know the kind where you got a better birthday gift than you asked for and the person that bought the gift says "but wait there's more", then pulls out a bonus gift. Yes, some things still haven't happened in my life as yet, such as me getting married or having my own home, but I have become confident that God will give me His best in His perfect timing.

If it is one thing that I want to leave with the person reading this testimony, it is that there is one thing that you can expect, expect God to surpass your expectations. Always.

–Antonique Etora Bullard

Chapter 2 Checklist

- ☐ Understand that expectations shapes your decisions

- ☐ Guard your heart against the wrong seeds of expectation

- ☐ Recognize the difference between human expectation and Godly expectations

- ☐ Do not make expectations your idol, but rather rely on God

- ☐ Complete exercise to determine how aligned your expectations are with God.

CHAPTER 3

Reality

Thinking Out Loud...

The expectations of life before 25 is so exhilarating. Reality, on the other hand, hmmmm not so much. The first four letters of reality is "REAL" and boy does it get real. For some reason, college was never a part of my plan for my life. I did not come from a family of college graduates and even though my mother always encouraged college, it was not mandatory. Due to this, I did not attend college until the age of 20. Even after enrolling, I still did not truly desire to be there and after 3 years, I decided I did not need it. Sure enough, I found myself heading for 25, college dropout, renting an apartment, minimal savings, and working at my families business. How did my life turn out like this? I mean I had so much dreams, so much talent, so much gifts, but at this point, my life surely did not reflect it. When I placed myself on the outside looking in, I began to look average and deep down inside, I knew I was not average. I just knew there had to be a greater plan for my life. This epiphany was my moment. Eventually, everyone gets there, but I just knew there had to be more to this.

While I did not act on this immediately, as months passed by this feeling grew stronger. As a former Christian living in a back slidden state, I knew what it was. I needed Jesus Christ to direct my path. My life was lacking purpose. I was lacking my whole reason for existence. No wonder I felt so lost.

> *Your word is a lamp to guide my feet, a light on my path.*
>
> *–Psalms 119:105 (NIV)*

You are around 25 now. You don't have that dream career you envisioned when you were 16. Or maybe you have not met that dream guy/girl you thought you would marry by now. That mansion you believed you would build doesn't seem anywhere near possible because you can barely keep up with your apartment rental payments. Everywhere you turn, reality is cornering you from all angles.

While reality often feels like a bolder in the gut, it is quite necessary when we are consistently walking along the wrong path. Despite the pain you may be feeling right now, know that it is not completely pointless. Anything that God allows, He will use for your good. He did not choose it, but he will use it.

> *And we know that all things work together for good to them that love God, to them who are called according to His purpose.*
>
> *–Romans 8:28 (KJV)*

Reality Develops Humility

One of the reasons reality is so necessary at this point in your life is because reality is humbling. Prior to reality setting in, often times, it is easy to have a 'know it all' attitude and to become completely arrogant. It is almost impossible for a 'know it all' to learn anything new because in their minds all the knowledge in the world already belongs to them. Before the Lord can truly direct your paths, first you must be in a state to receive that which He wants to teach you. You must become humble and submissive. To be honest, if an individual's life is perfect or turned out to be completely in line with certain expectations, more than likely that person would not take time to pray, seek God, or any type of guidance for that matter. Often times, the sting of reality humbles straight into the throne room of God. Ask yourself, how many persons do you know completely ignored God because life was fine and appeared to be living up to what they considered perfect expectations? Then, out of nowhere, a moment a tragedy struck. Almost instantly that person sought God. In other words, reality stung!

One of the major keys to getting pass the initial shock that happens when reality sinks in is to embrace the humbling process. Accept the fact that life is not perfect, therefore neither are you. Accept the fact that you have made some not so good decisions but this does not have to be your pattern for the rest of your life. You must remember that God knew that you would get to this point in your life before you even knew it. He knows every hiccup, every setback, every shock, and every thought. He had the solution before you even realized you had a problem.

How comforting! Embrace that one day this will all be a distant memory and The Lord is allowing you to be humbled so that He can mold you. One of the greatest mistakes made by so many persons is that rather than becoming humble, some people decide to fight it and try to prove that despite their current reality, they can figure it out doing the same thing.

The sad part is that the humbling process will continue and this person will go through the same test until finally a decision is made to pass the test. It is that person's choice as to whether the cycle will continue for 5 more days or 5 more years. Passing the test is by allowing God to mold and alter your reality. Albert Einstein defines insanity as doing the same thing over and over again and expecting different results. Allow your reality to humble you so that the Lord can use you.

Reality Births Evolution

The beauty of life is its variety. Every person's reality is different. As a matter of fact, your reality is a big part of who you are as an individual. The reality for one woman may be that she is a single mother. Naturally she becomes very independent because her reality has shaped her into this person. On the other hand, your reality may be that you are a college student living with your parent/s, therefore your character traits may be more dependent. Once again, you see how reality shaped you into those traits of dependency. Since your reality is so embedded into shaping your character, it is safe to say whichever direction that reality goes in can shift your character in that same direction, whether good or bad. This is why it is so important to allow the Lord to shift your reality in the best direction possible. You may be wondering; how can the Lord shape my reality? I need you to understand that opportunities do not just strike by coincidence or happenstance. It is the Lord that opens and closes doors in your life. It is Him and Him alone that can shift your situations and circumstances in the blink of an eye. God can do more for you in a second than you can do for yourself in a lifetime. Now I'm not saying that the Lord will snap His fingers and you will live in a magic land where everything falls perfectly in line, although I'm pretty sure He has the power to do so. What I am saying is as discussed, the Lord will guide your life and decisions while he opens the doors and takes you to new levels.

As you make up your mind to allow God to shift your reality in a better direction, you will see that you will begin to evolve into a better version of yourself. You will see your circumstances such as better grades in college, better job opportunities, peace of mind improve and you will become motivated to both maintain this better reality and excel even higher. This is how evolution and growth takes place in life. Even through the pain of what your life may presently look like, know that on the other side of pain, God will carry you to the best version of yourself. When you finally do evolve, you will thank God that the sting of your reality placed you in the position to evolve.

Reality Breeds Connections

Reality, no matter how dark it may seem, also connects. However your life may look at the moment, what you are going through can connect you to so many others. You may notice that persons with similar experiences in life tend to gravitate towards each other, especially when they choose to share those experiences. Married women and men will likely connect with other married women and men. A person who is abused may connect with someone else who has experienced abuse. I choose to believe that the Lord brings those who have experienced similar adversities together to lean on each other for support.

As bad as it may seem, your current reality can be used to encourage others. You may be surprised how many persons may be observing your life and admire that in spite of your struggle, you are exuding strength. The fact that you are able to press on is the reassurance that someone else needs to know that God can also give them the strength to get through their reality. There is a connection taking place when similar realities collide.

Reality and Expectations Connect

As previously discussed, your expectations lead to the types of decisions that you make. Your reality is more often than not a result of a "series of decisions." Therefore if you make bad decisions, your reality will be bad and if you make good decisions your reality will be good. Of course there are always exceptions, but this is the typical rule of thumb. In order to buy a home or start a business, normally a person will have to save. That person would make a series of decisions to sacrifice fancy vacations, extravagant meals, and certain types of recreation, in order to save towards this goal. By making this series of decisions, that person's reality will be becoming a home owner or a business owner. On the other hand if this person decided to make the opposite decisions by going on fancy vacations often, eating steaks and lobsters impulsively, and engaging in every type of recreation despite the cost, the reality of being a home owner or business owner would more than likely not come to pass. Your decisions hold power to your reality! Since our decisions affect our reality and expectations affect our decision, you can also conclude that your expectations also affect your reality.

I did not have any expectation to complete college because I was not interested and sure enough, it became my reality, for the moment. As I took steps to rekindle my relationship with the Lord, He began to minister to my heart and show me that I can expect great things for my life. He reassured me, despite the way my reality seemed, if I trusted Him, He would turn things around. Of course I didn't believe it for a while but the Lord continuously told me to go back to college and complete my degree. He placed a deep gut feeling in me and also used other persons around me (prophetic voices) to confirm this continuously. Yes, I was pretty stubborn! After a while, I figured what do I have to lose? After almost 2 years of dropping out of college, I decided to go back to complete my degree. I made a decision that would enable the Lord to shift my reality.

My expectations were also different. Normally I got average grades and did just enough to pass. My motto was "C's get degrees". This time, the Lord transformed this mediocre mindset. He showed me that GREATER was in me. I embraced this new expectation and my first semester back to college, I finished the semester with a 3.98 GPA. Surprise, Surprise, God was right all along!

The relationship between expectation and reality is also a two way street. Not only do your expectations affect your reality, but your current reality then affects your expectations. Thus the cycle continues. Perhaps you may be from a low income family and your reality is that you will not be able to afford college. Due to this, you have no expectation of completing college. Maybe you come from a family of single women/men and this may be your reality, so your expectation is to never get married. No matter how you look at it, your current situation will have an impact on your expectations and your expectations will continue to impact your reality.

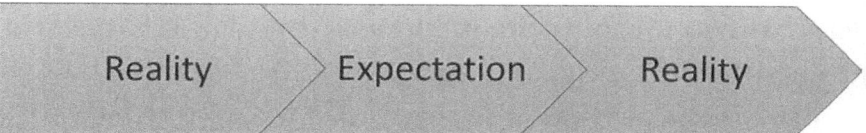

For me, since achieving such a high GPA (a new reality), my expectations changed. My new reality developed new expectations. I knew I could not go back to my old reality of making lower grades because I expected better for myself. In the end, I went on to graduating on the Presidents List and obtaining my Bachelor's degree with honors. It all happened because I obeyed the voice of God and as a result, a ripple affect occurred. My reality began to shift!

For every person, reality can mean several things. For some it may be heartbreak, loss of job, loss of a loved one, loss of self- esteem, a sense of worthlessness, feelings of depression, suicidal thoughts, or in my case, a feeling of purposelessness and emptiness. The most crucial step is recognizing this feeling and to act on these feelings by seeking the remedy. No, everything will not fall together perfectly or overnight, but no solution is overnight.

When you become sick physically, you seek medical attention and the doctor prescribes medicine for a period of days and in severe cases, months. You have to actively take these medications daily and eventually you will begin to grow stronger. While Jesus can most definitely provide instant healing, it is ultimately up to you to seek daily medication (His Word) and remedies (Seeking Him) in order to become strengthened. Just as the doctor specifically prescribes the medicine to your particular ailment and dosage according to you, The Lord will provide specific words to your situation and communicate with you in His special way. No two journeys are identical. Although realities can be harsh, there is no reality that Jesus Christ cannot change.

One of the greatest stories of a sudden shift in reality is the story of King Hezekiah. Hezekiah was a king that was a good man in the sight of the Lord. He followed Gods commandments as best as he knew how. Now Hezekiah became terminally ill. The Lord then sent the prophet Isaiah to Hezekiah to tell Hezekiah to get his affairs in order since he was going to die. When Isaiah left, Hezekiah prayed to God reminding God of the life he lived before Him. Hezekiah wept. The Lord was touched and ultimately added 15 years to Hezekiah's life. Not only did he add 15 years to his life, he would allow Judah, Hezekiah's kingdom, to win the war against Assyria. As a sign of all this, God promised to reverse the shadow of the sun dial (time). The Lord kept all three promises and it was so. (Isaiah 38:1, 2 Kings 20:1)

Hezekiah's reality was that he was extremely ill and he was going to die. This is probably the worst sting of reality that anyone can get. Just like many, Hezekiah anticipated a very different hand from the one he was dealt. Rather than sulk and just continue on with his death sentence, Hezekiah sought God in the midst of his pain. He prayed, wept, and asked the Lord questions. As a matter of fact, due to Hezekiah having relationship with God, he was able to remind God of how faithful he was to Him. AFTER seeking the Lord, God completely changed his reality and added 15 years to Hezekiah's life. God even gave him a bonus of winning yet another war. Death was a door that only the Lord could close. This was a reality God **alone** could shift, but it was Hezekiah's decision to seek God that led to this shift in his reality. It was this decision that allowed the Lord to close deaths door.

During this Quarter-Life Crisis, this is a decision making point. Are you going to continue a life in your current reality or are you willing to create a new reality with Jesus. In order to allow God to create a new reality, as He did with Hezekiah, there are several steps to take.

1. You must first be willing to rid yourself of your understanding and intellect. God's ways and your ways are not the same therefore if you try to understand Gods plan, you will never get it. Point, Blank, Period. It is imperative that you relinquish the desire to know every step of your life and how everything is going to work out. Three words, "Let it go!"

2. You must be fully convinced that your reality can change. Do not get caught up in thinking that you are stuck and you will always be stuck. Embrace Jesus because He is able to change any reality. He knows exactly which doors to open and

which doors to close. You will need His guidance in every decision of your life if you plan to truly make a change.

3. Once you have given God the complete guidance in your life, you also have a part to play. It is up to you to reorganize your life.

- This will include removing time wasters. Time wasters can be anything from social media to people. There is a big difference between being productive and just being busy.

- You must also make time to hear the Lords voice so that you can take steps in the direction of His plan for you. If he has directed you to go back to school, fill out the registration form. Perhaps he is pulling you towards a new career, research this career. Whatever it may be, begin making steps towards what God has told you to do. There is always a blessing on the other side of obedience.

- Finally remove toxic people. You know! The people that God has been tugging on your heart to separate from. Maybe it's that gossiping friend or that promiscuous friend. You will have to remove yourself from any environment that will hinder the shift in your reality from taking place. The truth is toxicity will destroy you and if you do not remove yourself, the Lord may decide to remove you anyway.

4. Two words, Trust God! No it will not be easy, but it will always be worth it.

Testimony Corner

The topic given to me was very difficult to write. Expectation vs. Reality. What did I expect in life and what was the reality of that expectation. I am 24 years old and will be 25 in a few months. I am a Christian, I have an incredible husband, and we have one daughter. Fortunately, I am surrounded by loving family and friends. I attend university, where I am currently pursuing my career in nursing. The Lord has been awesome to me and I thank him for his many wonderful blessings. At this age many people do not establish any of these things until much later in life, and often times not at all. So how did I end up being where I am?

Firstly, I had to let God LEAD my life. You must allow God to lead your life and I mean give it to him. He must be your guide and your conscience. Jesus has to be your "go to guy". Once I allowed Christ to be the head of my life he has been driving my ship. I did not expect to accomplish any of these accomplishments in the short amount of time that I already have. Honestly I did not even know if I wanted any of these things for myself, but the reality is that God does everything in his OWN timing. The problem is so often, we think we can tell God what to do. It is nice to have goals and dreams yes, however God may not release your harvest at 18,

19, or even 20 years old. Truthfully a lot of us are not yet even RIPE to receive Gods full blessings. This is why many people in their early 20's feel as if they have wasted this portion of their lives.

Secondly, we must live to please God. This was hard for me. A lot of people look at me and think I am the perfect Christian model. This is so far from the truth. I am not perfect and I have many flaws. Many times I would spend the whole day not praying or not reading my Bible. There was even a phase in my life where I had an ongoing battle with fornication. 1 Corinthians 6:9 Know ye not that the unrighteous shall not inherit the kingdom of God?…But if we want to live pleasing to God, how can we if we don't meditate on His word and seek Him daily in prayer. How can we please him when we give in to the desires of the flesh? I had to repent and ask God to forgive me. I asked God to constantly wash away my sins. And guess what, He did. I started praying more and mediating on His word. This was how I got to know God better. He knows the desires of our hearts, and once you commit to Him, He will provide for you. Matthew 6:33 But seek ye first the kingdom of God, and his righteousness: and all these things shall be added unto you.

Thirdly, obedience is very important to God. We must have a listening ear and a willing spirit.

Many times God wants to move in our lives but we just do our own thing. There was a particular issue that God was convicting me about and I did not want to listen. It was a battle with God on one side telling me if you love me then you will keep my commands and I am on the other side saying that "God this is not the norm that everyone is doing!" Matthew 7:14 But small is the gate and narrow the road that leads to life, and only few will find it. My stand is that if God tells you to do something (God's word lines up with the Bible so you will know it's really Him), then trust and believe that He knows what he is doing and faithfully do it. There is a special connection when a person is in Christ. Our wishes and desires and expectations for our lives end up being what God wanted for us in the first place! God takes our expectations, and he makes them our realities, but only when they are in alignment with His will. So therefore, if our lives are not where we expected them to be, that's fine. It's ok! In reality we may be right where God needs us to be for him to be able to use us. Glory and honor be unto the King!

–Mia Pierre-Louis

Chapter 3 Checklist

☐ The purpose of reality is to humble, birth evolution, and build connections with others.

☐ The decisions you make has the power to affect your reality, but only God can shift your reality

☐ Expectations and reality have a relationship that goes two ways. They both affect each other.

☐ Seek the remedy for shifting your current reality. Jesus is the remedy!

☐ Do your part and reorganize your life.

PART TWO

Hinderances

CHAPTER 4

The Past

Thinking Out Loud...

One of my past hurdles that affected me the most, even at the age of 25, was the lack of a father figure. Although my mom was an amazing single mother that provided well financially, I often yearned for a father. I would watch as other children at school have fathers pick them up, listen as they spoke about their fathers being a disciplinarian, or daughters talking about date nights with daddy. I watched and admired posts on Facebook on father's day and I often yearned to tell my own father's day story.

This feeling of rejection and abandonment from my father haunted me well into my 20's. So I did what I thought was best. I did everything in my power to bury them. Anything was better than actually feeling, even if that meant being numb. I would say things like, "I don't have a father" or "I don't know him" all because I hated being reminded of the rejection. Truthfully, the more I ignored it, the more it resurfaced. It resurfaced in my thoughts towards men. It resurfaced in my actions in relationship. It resurfaced in my self-worth. No matter how much I accomplished, subconsciously my past kept screaming loudly, "If you were good enough, he would have never left."

Now you are 25. You are officially legal to do everything your heart desires. I mean you are liberated in every sense of the word. Right? But wait! Time and time again, your mistakes visit you… over…and over… and over. You think about what you could have done differently. Maybe if your parents tried a bit harder. If only you had left that relationship when you knew you were supposed to. Perhaps you should not have dropped out of school. You never should have touched that drug. If only you could change that one decision in time, you just know that your life would be better.

Now the visitations from your past have become so frequent that it does not even fall in the category of visitations anymore. You find yourself in the past more than the present and in fact, you are now living there. The lines have officially been blurred. You can no longer distinguish the difference between who you were, who you are now, and who you are meant to be.

What if I told you this was all one big master plan by Satan himself to keep you from moving forward? At this very moment, you are carrying about 25 years of history. You have lived at least 9,125 days or 219,000 hours and the reality is some of your experiences are not good. Now the enemy has placed a magnifying glass on everything that was, in order to distract you from what is or what will be. He has deliberately kept you on rewind until all you can see is what did not work out, the person that hurt you the most, the life you did not have. Without even realizing it, you are being attacked from every direction and you don't seem to understand why stagnation is taking place.

That stagnant feeling is no coincidence. It was strategically planned by your enemy using the age old battle strategy. Surround your opponent until they are backed into a corner and have nowhere to turn. Unfortunately, your very own past is the secret weapon. Your history is attacking your present. While the attacks may appear in a physical form, it is not physical. The first blow thrown successfully hit your inner man and now your outer man feels it.

The Triune

The human being is a triune consisting of spirit, soul, and body.

> *And the very God of peace sanctify you wholly; and I pray God your whole spirit and soul and body be preserved blameless unto the coming of our Lord Jesus Christ.*
>
> *−1 Thessalonians 5:23(KJV)*

The soul comprises of mind, will, and emotions. It is who you are. The spirit, on the other hand, is your connection to God. It is how you communicate with God. The body is simply a shell that enables you to see, hear, taste, smell, and feels in the world as you know it. It has no conscious or mind of its own. A man's soul is eternal, the spirit comes alive when he/she accepts Jesus Christ, and your body ultimately dies.

The enemies primary goal is to severe the relationship between man and God. This leads to a spiritual death. Since the soul is where mind, emotions, and will resides, this is Satan's first point of attack. Ultimately, this leads to starvation of the spirit and the body just follows the leader.

The Attack on the Soul

As you know, your soul comprises of your mind, will, and emotions; however emotions will be the central focus for the moment. Since your soul is where your emotions come from, the state of your emotions affects the soul. If your emotions are in turmoil, then you can say your soul is not in the best state. Your soul is not just some big ball of emotions but it is also the connection between your body and spirit.

If the soul is in a poor state, the communication between spirit and body is also jeopardized. This is why when you are sad, you may find it hard to pray. Your sadness or feelings (soul) is preventing you (body) from prayer (spirit). When your bruised feelings (soul) prevent you from feeding your spirit, your fleshly desires become stronger. But here comes trouble and lots of it! Your body (flesh) ought not to do what it wants because this leads to spiritual death. This is exactly what your enemy wants. He will target your soul first. He will try to break the soul down as much as possible and deliberately use your past to do it. He wants to starve your spirit until it is dead.

> *For to be carnally minded is death; but to be spiritually minded is life and peace.*
>
> –*Romans 8:6 (KJV)*

For some, the past is extremely painful and the scars emotionally seem inconsolable. While scars are a part of life, the problem exist when the scars are not healing. Even with physical scars, if a scar is not healing, this can lead to infections that overtake the entire body. Any time healing does not take place, there is room for an environment of decay. You may wonder, what can possibly prevent my emotional scars from healing? Well, when your past is on replay in your life, you will not heal. Picture a wound that is constantly being touched over and over again. As much as the body is designed to heal itself, that wound will take a long time to heal and even when healing takes place it will not heal as well as it should. If you find yourself constantly thinking about the past and each time it is played, you get overly emotional, then you know that healing has not yet taken place.

Now let's talk about the mind. After emotions, the mind is the next part of the soul that is under attack and it further weakens the connection between spirit and body. Our emotions persuades our mindsets. Think about it! You may have made plans to go to the movies, but since you are **feeling** layed back or lazy that day, your **mind** changed. Let's go a little deeper. Perhaps you were in love before and you experienced heart break. You meet someone that seems to be ideal for you, however you change your **mind** because your **feelings** are still hurt. So now you can see whether you realize it or not, your perception (mind) is changed due to your emotional state. Once you allow your feelings to continue to persuade your mind then your soul will move further into a distressed state. Inevitably your will, will follow suit and your soul has successfully been wounded. At this point, the connection between your spirit and body has severely been weakened.

Starving the Spirit

Every human being possesses a spirit. However a person that has not accepted Christ is spiritually dead since the very purpose of the spirit is to connect to God. Nonetheless, this does not negate the fact that everyone on this earth is a spiritual being.

> For as the body without the spirit is dead, so faith without works is dead also.
>
> −James 2:26(KJV)

The spirit is a higher being than the flesh. When the soul becomes wounded, the spirit also becomes weakened because it will likely no longer be fed as it used to be. The spirit is fed through prayer, reading Gods word, fasting, and worshipping, simply because it was designed to stay in connection with God. The more these activities are neglected, the weaker the spirit will become and when the spirit is weak, this is the time a greater level of attack takes place. As a matter of fact, the enemy is depending on you starving your spirit so that he can remind you about your past some more. At this level, he is using condemnation to do it.

Condemnation is one of the greatest tools used to suppress an individual's desire to feed their spirit. Merriam-Webster's dictionary defines condemnation as 'a statement or expression of very strong and definite criticism or disapproval'. To be condemned means to express strong disapproval, therefore an individual that feels condemned is in complete disapproval of his/her self. Imagine a person constantly disapproving and criticizing the person seen in the mirror and must live with for the rest of his/her life. Speaking from experience, that feeling is exhausting and the cycle is never ending. Here are some traits of condemnation:

- Condemnation constantly points out your flaws.
- Condemnation constantly tells you what you did wrong but offers no ideas on how you can make it right.
- Condemnation builds regrets in your life so that your spirit will die slowly.
- Condemnation tells you that not even Jesus wants you or can help you.
- Condemnation tells you that there is no redemption for you so you might as well not even try.
- Condemnation tells you that your past overrides your present and future.
- Condemnation tells you to give up on your spirit because you are not worth it.
- Condemnation tells you it's the end.

I'm being so descriptive of what condemnation is because I want you to recognize it in your own life. It is very real. Just like every other attack, condemnation is not from the Lord. Since these attacks are not from the Lord, He is able to destroy it in your life. Resist and refuse to believe those thoughts because they are all lies from the father of lies.

> *For God did not send his Son into the world to condemn the world, but to save the world through him.*
> *—John 3:17(NIV)*

The Body: Follow the Leader

At this point, the body has no choice but to follow the leaders. Remember the body is just a shell and does not have a mind of its own. Since the soul is weakened and the spirit is barely alive, it will show in actions which are expressed through the body. This can be anything from mannerisms, to attitude, to body language. By entertaining such thoughts of the past and not allowing old wounds to heal, an infection has spread through your being and can move on into the lives of others like a plague. The manifestation of your wounded soul and spirit is now happening through your body (actions).

Here is an example! There is a young lady that we will call Taylor. Taylor is used to being disappointed. Parents, friends, and family have always disappointed her. It seems as if the more she trusted them, the more they let her down. Since this has seemed to be the story of her life, Taylor always carries this underlying expectation of disappointment. The past is playing such a pivotal role on her perception. Taylor begins to materialize this belief in her attitude towards people. She refrains from asking for help and assistance from others, even when she feels led to. Even when it is necessary. As a matter of fact, even when help is offered to Taylor, she refuses help because she feels like she does not deserve it. Taylor figures she has always figured it out in the past and she will continue to do so on her own. Her actions have now morphed to suit her past experience. Not only are her actions affecting her, but they are affecting the persons around her by the way she interacts with them. If she is not careful, she will inflict hurt on those closest to her and thus the infection spreads like a plague.

Taylor is not alone. Like so many others, my past affected my future. I expected rejection in every aspect of my life and in no way did I ever think I would excel. This was in relationships with men, educationally, and spiritually. Unconsciously, my thought process was that if I was not good enough for my father, how can I be good enough for anyone or anything else? In relationships, I felt if my father never protected me, why would another man do it? Needless to say, my actions reflected this. I acted rejected and like a person that did not expect to excel.

When I truly gave my life to the Lord, He changed this perspective. The Lord showed me that there is new life in Him. That although I could never forget the past, that He would erase the pain and hurt of the past, but ONLY if I let Him. Not only would he erase the pain, guilt, hurt, and shame, but He would use my past to help others that are going through similar situations. One of my favorite verses that the Lord always reminds me of is:

When my Father and Mother forsake me, then the Lord will take me up.

–Psalms 27:10 (KJV)

What a loving reminder that despite what I went through, even if I feel like a rejected orphan, God will take care of me? The Lord shielded me from the attacks of the evil one until it could no longer harm me.

The Lord can also do the same for you. No, there is no time machine. The past cannot be undone, but healing and restoration can certainly take place. God is able to remove the pain that you are constantly feeling when you think about that old boyfriend or girlfriend. He can heal the pain you feel when you think about how your father or mother was not there. He will teach you how to release those who hurt you physically, sexually, emotionally, or any other way.

The Lord will not turn away your broken heart. Not only that, God can restore you. The beauty about restoration is once it has taken place, it feels as if the past hurt and pain did not even exist.

My sacrifice, O God, is a broken spirit; a broken and contrite heart you, God, will not despise.

–Psalms 51:17(NIV)

The Lord will also begin to show you who you really are through his eyes, so despite how you feel, you will know you are not condemned. As a matter of fact, once you have already given the Lord your life, there is no condemnation and your spirit can begin to live again.

> *Therefore, there is now no condemnation for those who are in Christ Jesus.*
>
> *–Romans 8:1(NIV)*

Any thought that tells you differently is a lie. Not only is it a lie, but it is an attack! Now that you have recognized that it was all an attack to begin with, it is strategy time!

Confronting the Past

One of the hardest but necessary things to do is confront the past. Most people, like I did, try to sweep it under the rug and act like it never happened. 25 years of history goes unresolved and bottled up. Once you have given the Lord leadership of your life, you still have to confront those unresolved feelings so that true healing can take place.

You must believe that healing can take place. I mean not just say that you believe it, but really believe it from your heart. There are so many others like you that had a bad past, that have been hurt, but the Lord was still able to use their lives for His purpose. There are so many persons the Lord has used for His glory despite their broken past that it may seem unbelievable. As a matter of fact, as you read Gods word, you will see he usually uses persons with less than stellar backgrounds, cleans them, molds them, changes them, and then uses them. Moses is a perfect example of this.

Everyone knows the story of Moses and how he delivered his people out of Egypt, however many forget why Moses left Egypt in the first place. Moses murdered an Egyptian and when Pharaoh found out, he ran for his life. In other words, Moses was a murderer. Now let us think about this in terms of our society. A young man which was lovingly adopted into royalty as a prince ends up killing one of the civilians in the kingdom out of anger. I am sure if that happened in our world today, many would be outraged, write him off, and see him as nothing more than a criminal. Imagine the social media posts, the headlines, the scandals, the outcries! Undeniably Moses made a big mistake and was disobedient to God, however the Lord did not condemn him.

Instead, the Lord guided him and used him to deliver the people of Israel. I am pretty sure there are many others with "better" backgrounds, however the Lord still chose Moses. God is not hung up on your past mistakes and no matter how badly you think you messed up, he is able to heal you and use you. Just as Moses, greatness lies in your future and not your past.

Next you have to speak to your past situation. Yes, you read that right! Speak! There is so much power in the tongue.

> *Death and life are in the power of the tongue: and they that love it shall eat the fruit thereof.*
> *–Proverbs 18:21(KJV)*

Use that tongue to decipher what you want to live or die in your life. You have the authority to decide if hurt, pain, and rejection will continue to live from your past. Speak what you desire to see into existence. Put that past on notice that you have released it. Say this out loud.

"I _____ renounce any past hurt in my life. I release anyone that has hurt me, in the name of Jesus. I renounce every feeling of rejection. I take every thought that is not in alignment with what God says about me captive and make it obedient to Christ. Past, you will no longer seep into my future. I am a new creature in Christ Jesus and old things are passed away. I am free from condemnation in Jesus name."

Ok! So that was the practice run! Say it again but this time, like you actually believe it with your whole heart. Say it with authority and life as if you are snatching something that was stolen from you. Snatch back your happiness! Snatch back your peace! Snatch back your future!

"I _____ renounce any past hurt in my life. I release anyone that has hurt me, in the name of Jesus. I renounce every feeling of rejection. I take every thought that is not in alignment with what God says about me captive and make it obedient to Christ. Past, you will no longer seep into my future. I am a new creature in Christ Jesus and old things are passed away. I am free from condemnation in Jesus name."

This is not the only words of declaration you can make over your past. Ask the Lord to guide you into declarations that may be more specific to your situation. Oh and trust me, He will lead you!

Wait a minute, you are not quite done yet. That was just the foundation. Now that you have established belief and declared your healing, here are four steps that you can use to overcome through the blood of Jesus Christ.

1. Confess the pain and hurt

There are so many persons that are going through hurts and pains but prefer to bury those feelings. You may be one of those persons and each day you paste this perfect smile on your face. If only someone could hold a spiritual x-ray over your heart, it would be evident that the many scars from your past has your heart black and blue. You constantly weep when no one is looking because of the intensity of this pain. The Lord wants your confession. While He is all knowing and already knows the state of your heart, He wants you to communicate it to Him. This confession can be verbal, in your heart, or even through weeping. You may be thinking, why does the Lord want my confession? The confession is not for the Lord, but it is to provide a release for yourself. No longer will you have to walk around pretending that everything is okay, because frankly it is hard work. As you become vulnerable and honest before the Lord, you become naked (emotionally) before Him. At this point, He is able to truly step in and healing can begin.

2. Accept the past

No matter how much you try to change it, the past is permanent. There is no way that it can be changed. I am truly sorry that those things happened to you. I am even sorrier for the pain you are going through, but know that although the past cannot be changed, the Lord will turn it around and make it benefit you. In this moment, you may be thinking how can all the terrible things I have done benefit me?

Trust the Lord beyond your understanding. Know that, your mistakes are now a part of your history.

Meditating on God's Word (The Bible) will help you to find peace. God's Word helps you to see and understand the way the Lord views you. As you begin to read it consistently, you will begin to see yourself through the Lords eyes and before you know it, the big mistakes you have made will not seem so big anymore. You will realize that God is much bigger than those mistakes. He is so great that even your mistakes must bow to Him! He will give you peace.

3. Forgive

Reading Gods word will not only give you peace, but it will allow you to get to know God. His words will allow you to learn of His characteristics. We are made in the image of God therefore we have traits and characteristics of God. He is loving, kind, merciful, loves order, just, and forgiving. As you develop in the Lord, His desire is that your characteristics become like His. He wants you to forgive. You may be saying, how can I forgive someone that has mistreated me? Even worst, how can I forgive someone that has not even bothered to apologize to me? How can I forgive someone that is not even aware that he/she has hurt me? How can I forgive someone that does not even care? Forgiveness is not conditional on the other person. Despite what you have been taught, forgiveness is not something that should be earned by a person, but we should practice freely forgiving those around us because it frees our heart. Forgiveness keeps our hearts pure before the Lord. Whether this person wants it or not forgive them. There is a saying that says, "Holding on to anger is like drinking poison and expecting the other person to die." In other words, unforgiveness hurts you more than the person. God forgives us despite what we have done. He does not count the times our actions have hurt Him. You and I must forgive as we expect to be forgiven.

4. Let Go

Now it is time to let it go. The misconception that many people hold is that letting go is a one-time thing. While that is a beautiful thought, it could not be further from the truth. It is unlikely that you will let go of 25 or more years of history in one day. Each day, you have to make up your mind that you will not move backwards. You will not return to your past. You have already let it go. As you consciously make this decision, healing will take place day by day. Time will do its job and heal your wounds. There are times the past will try to resurface, however you must stand firm on the word of God. Continue to believe, declare, confess, accept, forgive, and let go.

Time is non-existent to God. It is completely irrelevant. God does not see you in past, present, or future. He sees you as who He has called you to be. No longer should you allow the past to add to the growing pains of 25. Let the Lord do the work for you, He is able.

> *Now unto him that is able to do exceeding abundantly above all that we ask or think, according to the power that worketh in us.*
>
> *–Ephesians 3:20 (KJV)*

Testimony Corner

After graduating high school, I did what everyone expected me to do and go off to college in the USA. I was 17, only Bahamian at my school, never been away from my family, wanting to please everyone, and wanting to fit in. I had the "college experience". At home, I had male friends who I knew from primary school, so being naïve I thought all men knew how to be just friends with females. One evening during my first term I went to one of my male "friends" dorm room to study for a test so I thought- my "friend" had other plans. Before I knew it I was fighting him off me. I was able to escape without any injuries or physical damage. But what I didn't realize was the emotional and mental injuries. I kept it a secret because I thought I should have known better and that maybe I led him on. I started to party; I had multiple sex partners and started drinking although I didn't start drinking until I turned 21. I was afraid of going to jail in the next man's country. Each semester I returned to campus, my partying increased. At one point having multiple partners started to take a toll on me so I decided I would be celibate. But I continued to party and drink. My partying and drinking got so bad that there was a semester that I was drunk every day of the week except Tuesday and that was because it was the only day that there wasn't a party happening. I dropped out of school- more accurately I flunked out of college and returned home. I wasted my time and my parents' money. I came home and had to deal with my shame, low self-esteem, and depression without the help of alcohol. I couldn't disguise these emotions with alcohol after all, I was now back home, people not only knew me, but knew my parents. I couldn't embarrass them and I couldn't handle the looks and lectures from my parents when I came home drunk. So many nights I wanted to leave this world, I was depressed and suicidal. I battled depression and I mastered the art of hiding my pain behind my pretty smile. I thought I was trapped in my mess.

I am an overcomer!

But God…

I gave my life to the Lord many years ago and was a chronic backslider because I didn't know how to let go of my mistakes. I constantly felt like a failure and God's mercy was too good for me because I would waste it like I did when I was in college. A year ago I decided to completely submit to God everything the good, the bad, and the ugly. The process hasn't been easy but I have seen the transformation. I have learnt to love myself the way the Word of God describes love. I learnt to be patient with myself, to be kind to myself, to be slow to anger with myself and stop recording all my wrong doings. I accepted the fact that God's love frees us from condemnation and that He loves me regardless of my sinful nature. The more I read the Word of God the more I understood the nature of God. Like the song writer stated… the more I seek Him the more I find Him, the more I find Him the more I love Him. So now when the devil tries to condemn me with my past and entangle me with the heaviness of depression, I seek God. I go to His Word. I remind myself that I am a new creature in Christ Jesus. I start to declare the Word of God over my life and put every thought under subjection under the Blood of Jesus. I no longer hide my battles especially if I feel overwhelmed by it. In these vulnerable moments, I seek assistance and prayers from my friends. I know that God will provide me with the people and tools to not only fight, but to win every battle presented by Satan.

–Lesley Cover

Chapter 4 Checklist

- ☐ Recognize the attacks on the soul, spirit, and body

- ☐ Confront the past

- ☐ Declare freedom

- ☐ Confess the pain, accept the past, forgive and let go

CHAPTER 5

The Void

Thinking Out Loud...

Truth moment! When I was a teenager, I partied a lot. I felt as if I had to find a party spot every single day of the week. Seven days! On days when there was no club opened, I literally felt upset that there was nowhere fun I can hang out. I thought, "What am I actually supposed to do at home?" Probably the right answer would have been homework but obviously I did not get that memo. Around this time of my life, nothing stopped me from clubbing and I do mean nothing.

So that meant if I had to hike rides with strangers, miss school the following day, or go at it alone, it did not matter. I just felt a need to be amongst the crowd, drinking alcohol, and dancing the night away. While the average teenager may crave to party, every day of the week was too excessive for any teen. At the time I did not realize it, but that need was being driven from somewhere. What I didn't understand was that there was a great big void in my heart and I was trying to fill it by partying. It was not until my 20's did I really begin to realize that my life was filled with so many voids and my behavior was only making it worst.

The word void can take on several different meanings, however in this case we will look at a void as a completely empty or vacant space. In addition to being an empty space, I envision a void as a deep dark hole that has no end. Unfortunately, from the outside looking in, it can appear to be a shallow hole, however once you are sucked in, the limitlessness becomes evident. The void is never *satisfied!*

Types of Voids

There are so many different types of voids that can exist in your life and it can come in so many different forms. You can experience a void of love, or a void of companionship, a void of hope, or a void of faith. In other words, you can experience an emptiness where love, companionship, hope, or faith would have existed. The catch 22 is often times, you can be yearning for these feelings or a void may be existing without you even realizing it right away.

Perhaps you are wondering, how do voids become present in my life? What have I done to create this bottomless feeling that just won't go away? The answer is, it is nothing that you have done but it has more to do with how you were created. As humans we are not designed to be empty. Our spirits are designed to have relationship with God, which is mediated by Jesus Christ, and filled with His Holy Spirit. The moment we negate from this design, there is a vacancy where the Holy Spirit should be. Remember a void is an empty space. This one vacant space or hole now produces several branches or voids. It is our relationship with God that gives us a sense of love, companionship, hope, faith, to name a few.

When He is missing, one branch appears. We can call it the void of hopelessness. Then another branch appears. We will call this one the void of faithlessness. Then another, the void of loneliness, and so on. This only leads to further emptiness. As mentioned before voids are bottomless or limitless so as time increases, you will feel like you are sinking deeper and deeper. This is why around the age of 25 when the feelings intensify, you begin to really feel and wonder what is going on? Chances are this void or voids always existed, but your feelings are unable to facilitate how deeply you begin to drown into this emptiness.

Void Fillers

The problem with any empty space is there is always something lurking to fill it. Remember, you and I are designed to be filled. An empty house will eventually be filled one way or another. Let's take a look at one of Jesus' parables.

When a defiling spirit is expelled from someone, it drifts along through the desert looking for an oasis, some *unsuspecting soul it can be devil. When it doesn't find anyone, it says "I'll go back to my old haunt". On return, if it finds the person spotless clean but **vacant**, it then runs out and rounds up seven other spirits more evil than itself and they all move in whooping it up. That person ends up far worse off than if he'd never gotten cleaned up in the first place.*

–Matthew 12:43-45(MSG)

Jesus was speaking to the Pharisees about a generation which was delivered from spirits, however when the spirits were driven out, there was an empty space left. Once this generation was delivered from the spirits, they did not become Holy Ghost filled and thus there was still a void. The vessel remained empty. The spirit recognized this vessel was still empty, so these spirits sought more spirits and consumed the empty vessel or space.

The reason the spirit sought more spirits is so that it would make it harder to be evacuated from that space again. It can be concluded that the spirit wants to get comfortable this time around with no intention of leaving. Similarly this occurs more than anyone would like to admit. Wherever there is a void, there are always the activities of evil spirits trying to fill these voids. Here is the clincher! Are you ready for it? THE open doorway, that let these spirits into your life to wreak havoc and destroy you, is SIN!

For we wrestle not against flesh and blood, but against principalities, against powers, against the rulers of the darkness of this world, against spiritual wickedness in high places.

–Ephesians 6:12 (KJV)

Have you ever wondered why persons that are depressed often turn to drugs and alcohol for comfort? The void of joy (absence of joy) leads to depression, which will be discussed in greater detail later in the chapter. So since the joy of the Lord is not present, that person yearns for something else to fill the space that joy would have occupied. This is when the temptation to sin will become heavy because the evil spirit is actively seeking to enter an open doorway in order to fill the empty vessel. The evil spirit attempts to open doorways through drugs, self-mutilation, partying, alcohol, ungodly relations, money, sex, and the endless list of sins individuals are tempted with. The problem is, the pleasures of temptation is just an illusion and these are all just temporary fills that always result in permanent consequences.

> For the wages of sin is death, but the gift of God is eternal life.
> –Romans 6:23(KJV)

There are times during worship or prayer that the presence of the Holy Spirit fills a room. It's the type of glory that cannot be put into words but the feeling is unmatched. It feels very much like a high and in that moment, nothing else in this world matters. Anything that the Lord creates, the enemy tries to duplicate and creates a counterfeit. This is why drugs, alcohol, and sex (outside of marriage) can all be associated with a "high". But unlike the Holy Spirit, it is all temporary. The more you engage in these temporary highs, you will always desire more to "fill" the void. Then again, the void can never be filled because it is endless. It is just a mirage.

The enemy uses a first high tactic to draw persons in. Once you experiment and indulge in the first high, you are compelled to try it again. You will always remember your first. The first time you had sex. The first time you got drunk. The first time you got high on drugs. But the reality is there is nothing like the first high. Each high after the first high is not as intense and many individuals will continue to chase after the intensity of the first high which will never exist again. So as one high ends, there is a constant pursuit of another high and thus a downward spiral commences. At this point, these evil spirits have successfully opened a door.

Consequences of Temporary Void Fillers

Voids often also interfere with your identity. Anyone that drinks excessively is referred to as an alcoholic. A person that loves money is called greedy. A person that regularly smokes is called a smoker. So in other words, you become identified by your habits. You are being called alcoholic, smoker, or greedy. Your temporary void fillers are now altering your identity because they are dictating WHO you are. Once you have accepted the fact that you are an alcoholic, sex addict, or drug addict, you begin to claim an identity that is outside of Gods will for your life. As a matter of fact, these void fillers are trying to become your god because they are telling you who you are and what you do. Anything that tries to rule you and tell you who you are is taking on a godlike role. Our Creator alone has legal authority to tell us who we are and rule over us. Anything else should never be accepted and EVICTED IMMEDIATELY. You are not an alcoholic because that is not your identity!

Sadly, it is not until you realize the void is bottomless and your identity has been misidentified that the expression of these voids begins to surface. This is when hurt, bitterness, anger, resentment, and depression often happens. At this point, most people come to the realization that possibly there is a problem. Perhaps a young man has been using multiple sexual relationships with women as a void filler for years. When he finally becomes numb and realizes that it is no longer "fulfilling", he may express it as bitterness towards women.

A woman in the same situation may use hurt as her expression. As for me, depression was the expression for my voids of loneliness because at that point, I grew bored with partying.

Depression

Depression has got to be one of the hardest feelings to combat. Depression makes an individual feel sad, lonely, rejected, lost, just to name a few. How do I know? Well I battled with depression in my 20's just like many others. The difference between overcoming and defeat in the battle of depression is the way an individual copes with depression. I chose to cope by sleeping excessively. Sleep felt like my only escape from the pain I was experiencing. I also isolated myself from friends and family. It felt bearable when I was among others, but when I was alone, I became extremely sad. Despite that, I still always wanted to be alone because I did not want anyone to sense that I was not okay. In the moments of loneliness various voices came to my mind. The voices would tell me, "You deserve to be alone." "You will always be unhappy", "You are not good enough." As I listened, it escalated to words such as, "No one wants you" "No one would miss you if you were gone" "You are just not important enough" "You might as well kill yourself" Yes! you read that correctly. My depressive thoughts turned to suicidal thoughts. Obviously my way of coping by sleeping and being alone was certainly not helping. During the times of darkness, I did not realize it, but the enemy was whispering lies to destroy me. The sad part was for quite some time, I believed every single word. I am grateful that I found the knowledge of truth, which is in Jesus Christ.

As you can see, from my experience, another cycle was taking place. The expression of depression now led to me re-enacting void filling activities (sleeping) since partying was not working anymore. But just like partying, it was done in hopes of experiencing release and fulfillment. I was in pursuit of anything to gain temporary relief from the dark cloud that was following me. Unfortunately, I soon found that the temporary climax or get away only led to a bigger crash and deeper depression.

During my first few months of allowing the Holy Spirit to fill voids in my life, I STRUGGLED to allow the Lord to take full control of my life. I cannot emphasized how hard that was for me. I was so used to filling voids the way I knew how (partying, drinking, sex, sleeping). To my surprise, even when I allowed the Lord to fill the voids, it was still hard. I still felt tempted to do things my way. The dark spirit of depression and company kept coming back to check if my house was still occupied with the Holy Spirit. Eventually, I realized there is no peace like the peace the Holy Spirit brings. Even though it was hard, withstanding the tests was completely worth it. Once you have been made whole, there is no desire to be broken again. Chose to be made whole despite the cost!

Currently, I am completely set free from depression. To be honest, I cannot pin point the exact day that I overcame, but I gave the Lord my life and it is His saving power that has set me free. In Him I found my purpose which is to help others, like you, by spreading His truth. You have the choice to experience freedom through Him. I now know my pain was not in vain. Now my former pain can be used to give God glory and help others to do the same. Am I perfect? No way! When my mind begins to wander and I recognize what is going on, I chose to pray. Praying to God will help replace dark thoughts with thoughts of purpose, love, and faith during times of depression or whatever else your expression may be. I also often research and repeat bible verses that relates to what I am going through. This verse is a personal favorite that speaks directly to my thoughts.

> *Casting down imaginations, and every high thing that exalteth itself against the knowledge of God, and bringing into captivity every thought to the obedience of Christ*
>
> *–2 Corinthians 10:5 (KJV)*

Praise and worship has also helped me to overcome. During times of extreme heaviness, I would play uplifting music that glorify God and I could literally feel the weight being lifted.

> *To appoint unto them that mourn in Zion, to give unto them beauty for ashes, the oil of joy for mourning, **the garment of praise for the spirit of heaviness**; that they might be called trees of righteousness, the planting of the LORD, that he might be glorified.*
>
> *−Isaiah 61:3(KJV)*

If you are reading this, and you know you are in a downward spiral or even a cycle of filling voids, I ask that you whole heartedly take a few seconds to pray this *prayer*.

Dear Heavenly Father,

I humbly ask that You would forgive me of all my sins known and unknown. I confess Jesus as Lord and Savior of my life and I believe that He died for me. I ask that You would forgive me for filling my heart voids with sins that do not please You. I know my heart is empty and I need You to fill it like only You can. I need You to heal every bit of brokenness, every hurt, and every pain. Heavenly Father, I ask from this day forward, you would help me to embrace all that Your void filling Spirit brings. Peace, love, joy, hope, holiness, purity, and wholeness. I ask that my heart will no longer be void but completely consumed by You. I thank You for making me who You purposed me to be. In Jesus name I pray, amen!

And just like that, the Lord is ready to fill and heal you if you sincerely prayed that prayer. Is it an overnight fix? No! Will you wake up after one prayer and feel completely free? No! But with consistent prayer and Gods love, you will wake up one day, like I did, look back, and realize the pain does not exist anymore.

King Saul was the first king of Israel. Saul was king for 40 years, however he was only anointed by God for two years. When the anointing left Saul, there was a void. Rather than repent and seek the Holy Spirit once more, Saul decided to operate as if nothing happened. His lack of repentance left a doorway for anger, pride, and jealousy to step in. Power was his temporary void filler. He was completely consumed by his desire for power (temporary void filler) and any threat of losing power led to anger and jealousy (expressions). There were times that Saul was willing to kill his only son Johnathan because he felt threatened that he would lose his power. In the end, because Saul relied so heavily on his pursuit of power rather than the Holy Spirit, this ultimately led to his death. As a matter of fact, Saul intentionally fell on his own sword because he would have rather died than for his enemies to capture him. Even when facing death, Saul still was prideful.

The truth is that walking with the Spirit of God in you is a JOURNEY. A journey is continuous. Therefore as Matthew 12:43-45 stated, the spirits will constantly return to see if the void has been filled. In other words, temptation will always be present and test you. Allowing the Holy Spirit to fill your voids is a daily commitment that you must renew each day. There is no quick fix, but there is a permanent fix. His name is Jesus Christ!

Testimony Corner

There are often times when life doesn't quite go as we expect or anticipate. Most of us have the natural ability to plan and have our lives mapped out. College, then marriage, then children, and then maybe decide to find out what we can do for God. What happens when that plan you have is nothing like what God intended for your life? It is usually during these times of disappointment that depression begins to take root. Thus putting distance between us and our Creator. I found myself in that place at a very critical time in my life. I had reached the age (25) that I had given myself for marriage, and guess what someone came. We got engaged and started planning the wedding. Exactly six weeks before the wedding, he called it off. Anger, Frustration, Shame, and mostly disappointment were my garments for about a year and a half. Long right! Since these became my garments, fellowship with God was non-existent. The feeling of emptiness during that time overwhelmed me. I even said I do not want another prophecy, (just dumb) because it was all lies. Even though I was so far from God and I felt disappointed by God (which makes no sense), He created me to worship Him. The worshipper in me felt lost beyond words during that time because I was missing something. The emptiness got so loud some days that when I screamed I couldn't even hear it. That season of my life had a level of confusion, feeling lost, displaced, like a misfit that it pushed me away from the things of God and the fellowship of God. But because worship was embedded in me, there was one night the Holy Spirit said "enough". I remember sitting in my room trying to find my way back. By singing (this is what I did, that was the sign between God and I that said let's talk), the Presence of the Lord came and filled my room in a way I've never experienced. It was at that time it felt like the Holy Spirit just massaged my heart and breathed life back into it. He said to me clearly "This was not designed to kill you but to build you, LET IT GO!" It was at that moment I felt the healing balm of Jesus sit on my heart. It took me a year and a half to understand that Gods plans for me always trumps my plan but most importantly, He uses the 'STUFF' of life to build us. He actually was not taking from me but he was really trying to give me something better.

–Audra Bain

Chapter 5 Checklist

☐ Recognize the types of voids

☐ Recognize how voids manifest in your life

☐ Understand how temporary voids fillers comes into existence

☐ Pray against temporary void fillers

CHAPTER 6

Fear

Thinking Out Loud...

One of the most intense fears I had, was a fear of being alone. I came from a line of single mothers that provided well for their children. While there is certainly nothing wrong with being an incredible super single mother, I did not necessarily desire to be single my entire life. For some reason, I felt like being single and being alone meant being lonely. In my mind, it was all synonymous. This fear of lonely led me to always feel the desire to have a relationship or companionship. It did not matter how good or bad the relationship was for me, I just knew I needed to have someone. There were times I would find myself dating or talking to a guy, knowing that there was no future, however I carried on because all I knew was I did not want to be alone. This did not just stop at relationships, but I also always longed for friendships. Anything to cure the lonely. I just wanted to feel a part of something, then maybe the loneliness would not feel so real. I allowed myself to have associations with persons that were not the best fit for my life. They were not bad people, but they were just not meant for my life. I found myself in situations where

I was a part of a crowd, but I still felt alone because I did not fit in that crowd. I was allowing my fear to push me into compromising my decisions. Even in making those decisions, there was no resolution to the fear I felt. I was in an endless cycle. The cycle went like this. I was afraid to be alone so I sought companionship; I got companionship and still felt alone, so once again, I was afraid I would always feel alone. How exhausting!

ou look outside and you see someone panicking. That person doesn't make a sound but the look on that face immediately tells you this person is in fear. Without even thinking, you can just tell, this person is petrified. There are so many persons living life in this same intense fear daily, however it is completely masked. Unlike the person outside, the look on their face does not give them away, but the fear still exist on the inside of them. If you were given a sneak peak of their hearts, you would clearly see fear sitting on a throne, ruling his/her life. Fear of failure, fear of loneliness, fear of the unknown, fear of trusting God, fear of releasing bitterness, and so much more, completely reigning the hearts of people.

> *Anxiety weighs down the heart, but a kind word cheers it up.*
>
> *–Proverbs 12:25(NIV)*

Fear and Decision Making

Should I stay in this relationship? Should I take my mother's advice? Should I give my life to the Lord? Should I listen to the opinions of others? The reality is, fear has affected the answers to so many questions, however it is one of the least talked about subjects. No one wants to admit to being afraid. No one wants to say, "Hey! I am afraid of disappointments, hurt, pain, rejection, or failure." Instead of verbalizing fear, most people suppress it as if it does not exist. The problem with suppressing it is, anything that is suppressed eventually spreads silently.

Fear carries certain traits. If your decisions mirror these traits, then more than likely, you are making decisions out of fear. The traits are as follows:

1. Fear does not allow you to think ideas through fully.
2. Fear feeds off of its own logic, whether it is right or wrong.
3. Fear accelerates the pace of decision making.

Think about it! Just like I was, you may be afraid of being alone. You begin to desire to have persons around you in order to suppress this feeling of fear. Unfortunately, due to suppression, the fear spreads. You do not think about your choices of associations fully. The logic of fear then says pick a friend, any friend, and you won't be so alone. This logic suggests that the type of friend does not necessarily matter, but you just need someone. As wrong as it is, it seems to make sense in those moments.

Since you believe this logic and do not want your fears to become a reality, you hasten your decision. You pick the first person you meet or have a conversations with longer than 5 minutes. Without testing this person's hearts towards you, you have already labeled that person as a friend, telling them all about your life. You have made a decision out of fear and decisions made out of fear are never the best decisions.

Someone else may be afraid of failure, therefore they do not think going to college or starting a business venture through fully. The logic of fear says, do something, anything. Just be "productive". Then this person quickly enrolls to some random degree program or starts this new random business.

There is absolutely nothing wrong with wanting friends, going to college, or starting a business, but the motive behind these ventures matter. I have a huge pill for you to swallow. Are you ready? ANYTHING done outside of the will of God for your life will carry consequences, no matter how good it looks or sounds. Sometimes it crashes and burns right away, other times it seems as if it is working for a while, but eventually you will realize it is not working out in your best interest. God's will, will always include what is best for your life. Therefore fear is a terrible motive and a horrible ruler that is never satisfied. Its loyal subjects are settling, regret, and sin!

> *LORD, I know that people's lives are not their own; it is not for them to direct their steps.*
> *–Jeremiah 10:23*

Fear Catapults Sin

Allowing fear to be the ruler of your life is a sure way to catapult you into sin. Let me clarify. I am not saying that if you feel afraid you will sin. I am saying if you allow fear to make decisions for you, then sin is sure to follow.

So you are 25 or older and you just cannot seem to find Mr. Right or get married. You then meet the most handsome guy you have seen all year and surprise, he is showing interest in you. The relationship progresses and you really like this guy, but uh oh, red flag! He wants to have sex before marriage. You promised yourself you would not go down this road again. Your next relationship is supposed to be your LAST relationship because you are just tired of the cycle. Furthermore, you just gave your life to Jesus and you have decided to abstain. Unfortunately, the ugly traits of fear begins to rear its head. You begin to think, suppose I lose this guy. This may be my last chance. I really want to get married. Maybe I should just do it this one time. Before you know it, you are giving in to fear. The problem is, if you give in to fear, you will sin.

When anyone acts out of fear, it is more likely to act in disobedience and ultimately sin is the product. It goes something like this. You become afraid, so you try to stop your fears from becoming a reality at all cost. This act of trying to prevent fear from becoming a reality results in disobedience to God. When you are disobedient, things start to fall apart so you become frustrated. As your frustration builds, your unbelief also builds and this all leads to recurrent sin. Sin is a fruit of fear.

Fear will not tell you to do what is right, because the goal of fear is to kill your faith. Fear will lean towards the easy decision which is usually not the way of God. God will take us down the narrow (hard) road, because He desires us to be dependent on Him. As stated, anything against Gods will is not the best decision.

> *Enter through the narrow gate. For wide is the gate and broad is the road that leads to destruction, and many enter through it. But small is the gate and narrow the road that leads to life, and only a few find it.*
>
> *–Matthew 7:13-14(NIV)*

Fear Immobilizes

Have you ever watched a scene in a movie where a person is about to get knocked down? I mean this person clearly sees the car coming but stays in place to be knocked down by the car. If you are anything like me, you yell at the television saying MOVE! But that person just stands there and gets hit by the vehicle. It was not until I had an experience of intense fear that I realized fear literally paralyzes. In the midst of fear, physically a person becomes immobilized.

As I continued to observe this trend, I realized people can also become immobilized spiritually when in fear. Physical fear is fleeting and lasts in the moment of attack or potential danger but spiritual fear is much slower to leave. Fear is a plan of the enemy that is often used to cancel our assignments or tasks that the Lord has given us. The voice of fear is very loud and will tell you, you cannot do what God has told you to do. It will tell you, you cannot stay saved, you cannot preach, you cannot abstain from sex, you cannot pray every day, or you cannot trust your spouse. This voice is like a scratched CD and will continue to speak for as long as you do not press stop.

The goal is to immobilize you and keep you in your current state. Obedience to God will propel you forward into a new state. If fear freezes you and your obedience, you will never get there. In other words, fear is seeking to steal your progress. It purposely prohibits growth so when you experience fear, almost immediately you know it is an attack from the enemy.

> *For God has not given us a spirit of fear and timidity,*
> *but of power, love, and self-discipline.*
>   *–2 Timothy 1:7 (NLT)*

The Lord tells you to leave that job because its season is up. He wants you to stay at home and strengthen your walk with Him because He is preparing you for full time ministry. What you do not know is full time ministry will propel you into a new state spiritually and financially. Fear will scream, "Are you crazy? How will you pay your bills? Where will you find the people for this ministry? You will be a joke." If you listen to fear, act in disobedience, and stay on that job, you will never experience true spiritual or financial freedom. On the other hand, if you are obedient, and move despite fear, you will experience all of the above and more.

Manifestation of Fear

The good news is that fear does not manifest overnight. Fear often starts out as doubt. You doubt that you will ever be happy so you become afraid of always being unhappy. You doubt you will ever experience true financial freedom so you develop a fear of poverty. There is a developmental phase. This phase can vary from person to person. Some persons have carried around seeds of fear since childhood that does not resurface until adulthood. Even as a child, these people may have made choices out of fear without even recognizing it. This was precisely my experience. As a child that observed my own family structure, I recognized I did not want the same structure for myself. As I got older and involved in relationships, doubt arose because my life seemed to be following the same pattern. Before I realized it, doubt developed into a fear.

This is not always the case, some fears develop in adulthood. Just like anything else, fear starts out in our hearts before the outward expressions begin. One way to stop these types of fears is to protect the gateways, to our hearts. More particularly, protect your ears and eyes.

Attachment to the wrong people is one major way our gateways are compromised. If you are around people that constantly speak words of fear, even if it's in their own lives, soon enough, you will develop this attitude of fearful thinking. As you also observe the results of their lives due to fear ruling their hearts, you will believe that these opinions were right all along. In reality, it was fearful thinking that led to those results. Be very careful not to assume that what has happened in the lives of others will automatically happen in your life. It does not matter how similar your situations may appear. Instead protect your heart so that your outlook and perception will not be tainted with fear.

Overcoming Fear

Faith in the Lord and His plans severely diminishes fear. You must understand that if the Lord told you to do something, the rest is not your business. How the Lord opens the door is not human concern, but obedience to walk through the door should be all we as servants are concerned about. When we learn to take the focus from details and focus on obedience, there is extensive room for faith. Faith will be discussed further in the next chapter. Just know that faith and fear cannot occupy the same space. Another reason faith in God is so powerful is because it takes the dependency from yourself. When you were a child, whenever your parents left you alone, you were afraid. But when they came back into the room or space, immediately you were not afraid anymore. This is because you depended on them to protect and comfort you. This is the same dependency the Lord wants you to have on Him. It is this dependency that will take away fear. He is with you therefore you have no need to be afraid.

> Give all your worries and cares to God, for he cares about you.
>
> *−1 Peter 5:7(NLT)*

During my Quarter-Life Crisis, I was not only afraid of being alone, but I was afraid of complete obedience to God. Complete obedience to God meant I could not have sex, drink, party, or curse. Because I did not know what a life like that would be like, I feared the unknown. In order to conquer my fear, I had to face it. I began to walk in the opposite direction than I normally would. Rather than making decisions to pacify and suppress fears, I eventually ran to it. I was willing to be obedient to God, and I was willing to try new things and be true to myself, even if it meant failure. I soon realized something quite interesting about fear. When fear becomes your reality, then fear automatically disappears. In other words, when you realize the thing that you fear so much is actually happening, there is no longer a reason to be afraid. Once I grasped this concept, I no longer held on to fear. I had to master the art of doing it afraid. So even when fear tells me not to open a business, I do it anyway, despite me feeling afraid. When it is already done, the fear goes away. One way to dethrone fear, is to reduce its power. This happens by facing it.

Gideon is a perfect example of someone that used these two steps to overcome fear. He depended on God and faced his fears. Israel was once again under oppression by Midian because of idolatry. The Lord sent an angel to Gideon to tell him he would be the one to set the Israelites free. Midian responded, "How can I rescue Israel, My clan is the weakest in the whole tribe of Manasseh, and I am the least in my entire family!" Gideon then went on to ask for a sign and the Lord gave him the sign as proof that He was truly speaking to Gideon. When it was time for Gideon to go to war against the Midianites, he called an army of 22,000 together, however the Lord said the army was too big.

The Lord then instructed Gideon to tell everyone that was afraid, to go home. This reduced the army by more than a half, however the Lord wanted a smaller reduction. Based on the way that the men drank at the stream, the Lord made the final cut. This time to 300 men.

When night fell, the Lord told Gideon to go down to Midians camp with his servant. He told Gideon that when he heard what the Midianites were saying, he would grow confident. Gideon did as the Lord commanded and went to the edge of the camp. He then overheard two men talking about a dream which signified that Israel would be victorious against Midian and all of its allies. Gideon went back to the camp and told his soldiers that the Lord had given Israel the victory. Needless to say, Israel won the battle and was indeed given the victory.

In this story, we see that Gideon's first response to the angel of the Lord was one of fear. Gideon felt like he could not complete such a big assignment and it was completely out of his league. When the Lord asks you to complete an assignment, it is much bigger than you. This is because if you can complete it all by yourself, you would not need God.

We also see God going completely against human logic. He told Gideon to make his army even smaller than it was. Imagine your country going to war and the leader saying the army is too big. You would probably assume he was losing his mind! God knew that if Gideon defeated the Midianites with so many soldiers, the Israelites would think the battle was won on human strength, rather than God. Once again, it can be seen that the Lord required total dependency on Him. Fear will always seek to steal that dependency.

Finally, before the Lord gave the Israelites the victory, fear had to be totally removed. First the Lord cut the army down by sending all the soldiers home that were afraid. He had to protect the soldiers that were not afraid from that contamination. Fear spreads, immobilizes, and kills progress so before it got any further, the Lord had to get rid of the people that were already being ruled by it. The Lord also had to remove fear from within Gideon, therefore he sent Him to the edge of the army camp in order to hear the discussion about the dream right before the attack could be made. Before Gideon could receive the victory, the Lord also had to rid him of fear. Despite having reliance on God, Gideon still had a role to play. He had to actually get up and do what the Lord told him whether he was afraid or not. Gideon had to face his fear in order to successfully complete the assignment that the Lord had given Him. In other words, Gideon did it afraid.

Fear Challenge

Let's try a fear challenge. On the next page, write down all of your fears. Every fear that you can think of.

If you are a visual person, you can use picture representations of the fears that you are experiencing.

Each day, tell the Lord that you cast that particular fear on Him and you will not carry it around. In moments when you begin to think about it again, remind yourself that you have already casted that fear on the Lord and it is no longer your problem. Do not give doubt a foothold in your mind because this doubt will soon develop into fear if you allow it.

In addition to this, make a conscious effort to do it afraid. If the Lord told you to write a book, even if you are afraid, just begin writing. If He told you to go back to school, even if you are afraid, fill out the application. If He told you to leave that relationship, even if you are afraid, break it off. Just do it afraid!

As you begin to see the Lord move in your life and you no longer feel afraid, cross that fear off of your list or take the visual representation down. Write down how you overcame. Was it the Lord that gave you a sense of peace as you casted that fear? Did He send a third party to minister to your heart? Did you just do it afraid and fear lost its power? However you overcame that fear, keeping a record of it will help you in the future whenever fear tries to manifest again.

Today before transitioning fully into the second quarter of your life, refuse to carry fear another day!

Testimony Corner

When I was asked to write on this topic of fear, I was at a loss because I said to myself 'I don't have any fears'. But the Holy Spirit said talk about your secret fear and how that affected your life. I was immediately reminded that as long as I could remember I had a fear of dying at the age of 25. Because of this, this fear affected me in ways that I didn't even realize. I took on risky behavior, got involved in drinking and partying so heavily that I was a borderline alcoholic. This fear paralyzed my life in that I didn't plan for the future because I didn't see myself as having one. I got so consumed with having fun before I died that there was no time for God. I was constantly chasing the next thrill, the next good time and why not? 'Mitiswelllive before I die' is what I thought. The enemy used this fear to manipulate me and keep me cut off from God and from having the life, the Abundant Life the HE came to give me. The enemy uses fear as a tool and a weapon and he did so masterfully in my life to the point I did not notice this fear at the forefront of my mind. Nonetheless, it affected every decision that I made. This fear almost became a self-fulfilling prophecy when at the age of 25, while seeking the next thrill at a club, I was stabbed multiple times and one of the stab wounds was in my chest.

It was almost like Job said; 'The thing that I feared has come upon me' but even on the hospital bed, with the doctors explaining the many ways I could have died, I still didn't turn to God. I continued to chase after the next cheap thrill. It wasn't until later that year while sitting outside at a party with a cup of liquor in my hand that I heard the voice of God say, 'What next will you put in front of me'? Right there! In that moment with my drink in my hand, I gave my life to Him, without a choir, no sermon or an organ, I put my faith in Him. While preparing to attend the funeral of three of my friends and just before my 26th birthday, a lady came up to me and told me that God said 'He moved my finished line, I was supposed to have died that month BUT because I put my faith in Him, He has given me another chance. What made this so impactful was the fact that I have never told another living soul of my fear of dying at the age of 25. God used the shield of Faith as a weapon against the fiery darts of fear that the enemy had released at me.

–Brian Bain

Chapter 6 Checklist

☐ Recognize how fear affects your decision making, catapults sin, and immobilizes

☐ Understand the manifestation of fear

☐ Tips on Overcoming fear

☐ Complete the Fear Challenge

PART THREE

Overcoming

CHAPTER 7

No Faith = No Results

Thinking Out Loud…

Even as a saved believer that absolutely adored Jesus Christ, I struggled with my faith. I would go to church on Sundays and sing the songs that described how great and faithful the Lord is. Believe me, in those moments of singing. I was being honest and sincerely wholeheartedly felt His faithfulness. Then life happened. When cash was low or a family member was acting up, I completely forgot how faithful I would proclaim God to be. I allowed my circumstances to tell me to feel worried or feel angry rather than believing that God would fix that situation. The hard pill to swallow is I did not truly have faith because if I did, my actions would align with what I believed. The thing that baffled me was that God had provided for me over and over again, but yet I always seemed to forget when a new problem arose. He never let me down before. He has shown His faithfulness towards me, even when I didn't deserve it, but here I was constantly questioning Him again. I was at a point where I had to figure out what was stopping me from truly having faith. I had to know what was really going on in this area of my life.

aith is such a heavy word that is used loosely. Whenever something terrible happens, you and I are always taught and told to have faith. No one ever takes into consideration the person's thoughts or feelings, but it is simply said, "have faith". It is as if by saying those two words, the person would magically be filled with faith and somehow their circumstances will be fixed. That is exactly how I felt. Quite frankly, sometimes hearing those two words became so exhausting and even annoying. There were times someone would tell me to have faith and I literally thought, "I don't want faith, I want results." I continued, "How long must I have faith for the finances to change? How long must I have faith that this relationship will make sense? I'm not seeing any results. How long? How long? How long?"

The mere fact that I asked this question means that I did not have the slightest clue what faith meant. The first step to having faith is to understand what the word faith means. This is how the Word of God describes faith.

> *Now faith is confidence in what we hope for and assurance about what we do not see.*
>
> *—Hebrews 11:1(NIV)*

This definition of faith needs to be broken down even further. There are three key words in this verse. Confidence, Hope, and Assurance. Merriam-Webster dictionary defines these words as follows:

- Confidence: reliance on another's discretion; a feeling or consciousness on one's [another person's] power.
- Hope: Desire with expectation of attainment
- Assurance: Security

So let's try to define faith again. Faith is having [reliance on Gods discretion] in what we [desire with expectation of attainment] and [security] about what we do not see.

Confidence

As you have just read, one part of faith is relying or having confidence in Gods discretion or judgment. Gods discretion is what God decides should be done in a particular situation. As difficult as it may seem, faith requires that you be fully persuaded and dependent on what God knows and feels is best. Your personal judgment can be easily converted and side tracked by feelings, among other things, however Gods judgment is always right. Just as any loving parent, He will desire the absolute best for His children and will make decisions with the best solution in mind.

This would also mean in order to accurately stand in faith for something, it must be in Gods will because part of the definition of faith is having reliance on what Gods believes is right (discretion). God's discretion WILL NEVER be out of His will. That is why a person standing in faith for another woman's husband makes no Biblical sense. This would violate the mere essence of what faith is.

Hope

The second part of faith is having hope or desiring with expectation of attainment. It is one thing to desire or want something, but it is another thing to want something and expect or believe that you will actually get it. You can see a new home and want that new home, however you may never actually believe that you will attain that home. This is why when you are having faith in anything; you must truly believe that you will get it. This second part will only make sense when the first part is already established. If you are dependent on Gods discretion and believe in what He decides for your life, then it will only make sense for you to expect to get what He decides for you. In other words, your dependency on God's discretion relates to how strongly you expect to attain these desires. Where there is little dependency (confidence), there is little expectation of attainment (hope).

Assurance

The third part of the definition of faith is the hardest one to follow. It is having security in what you do not see. I mean, it is so easy to believe what is seen. That's because even as children, we have all been taught to believe this concept. If you can see, feel, taste, hear or smell something, then without a question, you know it exist. Now if you cannot, then you should question its validity or possibility of existence. If you only have $2 in the bank, it means you have no money. If your father drinks then he is an alcoholic. If your marriage is falling apart, then it means you will get divorced. All of these examples will say, "Believe it because it is right in front of you."

This is why the Bible takes on a different definition and deliberately states to be secure in what you cannot see because what you cannot see, once again, requires you to rely on God. So you are 25 and you do not see how you will own a home. Faith! You do not see your marriage restoring. Faith! You have been trying for months or years but you do not see a positive pregnancy test. Faith! God is requiring you to be secure in what you cannot see. Being secure means being comfortable and sure. When a new homeowner secures a home with burglary bars, alarms, and dogs, they are not jumpy and afraid because there is a sense of security. These owners are not worried when they go on vacation, because the home is secure. This is the same sense of security the Lord desires for his children to have in the unseen. God does not want you to be worried but comfortable and secure.

Faith is:

1. Relying on Gods discretion
2. Desiring with expectation of attainment based on His discretion
3. Being secure in the unseen

After coming into the realization of what faith is, it is important to understand how to develop faith. It is one thing to be able to properly define what faith is, but it is another to actually develop faith. The key to having faith in anyone or anything is trust, you will never be faithful (full of faith) to anyone or even God if there is no trust.

You will only trust someone when you know them. Everyone has heard this statement at least once as a child. "Do not talk to strangers!" In other words, you are taught not to trust strangers. From childhood, you were wired to develop trust in persons when you get to know that person. How then can you trust God if you do not know Him? Sure, you can say because He is God and while that is true, trust will still fully develop the more you know His character.

The most effective way to get to know anyone is to talk to them daily. The more you talk to that person, the more you will understand that persons likes and dislikes. You will be able to seek that persons advice and counsel. As time progresses, he/she will begin to share their deepest secrets with you. Over the years, that relationship will grow and develop in honesty, beauty, trust, and faith.

Prayer and Faith

Prayer is communication with God. While there are various depths and different types of prayer, it all boils down to communication. Just like many, you may not pray because you feel as if you do not have the words to say, but just as any form of communication, start small. When you first met your best friend, you did not begin with lengthy conversations, however imagine if you had never started a conversation at all. What would your life have been like without that person? Prayer is so important in strengthening faith because it does a number of things. Prayer creates intimacy, direction, expectation, confidence, and security.

Persistently praying to the Lord will bring intimacy. When I first became serious in pursuing Christ, I set time out each day to pray quietly to the Lord. I would find an un-interrupted space, whether it was the bathroom, an empty room, or a little corner of the living room area. There were times I would wake in the wee hours when everyone was asleep so that I could be totally uninterrupted. In that quiet area, no matter how big or small, I would pour out my heart to the Lord. I did not have the fancy words or biblical verses down pack, but I just told Him what was on my heart. If I was hurt, I would be honest and say, "Lord I'm hurting" If I was angry, I would say, "Lord I'm angry" If I was discouraged, I would say, "Lord I'm discouraged". There were times I was a complete mess and I would just lay there crying. I mean it did not make any sense trying to hide my life or feelings from The Lord, because He already knew. Pouring out to Him was not for Him but it really was for me. In those moments, I was developing intimacy with the Lord. I was learning to trust Him. I was realizing that I could rely on Him any hour of the day and He would listen. He would be attentive to my cry. It has now become a daily routine to spend time in His presence, sometimes hours at a time. On days when I get caught up, I long for this inti-macy and feel incomplete without it. Prayer will bring you true intimacy. It is expected to trust someone you are inti-mate with and this trust will build your faith.

The eyes of the LORD are on the righteous, and his ears are attentive to their cry

–Psalms 34:15(NIV)

Prayer Brings Direction and Expectations

As you begin to communicate with the Lord, He will begin to speak. Prayer, just like any form of communication, is a two way street. Once you have spoken to the Lord, it is important to take time out to listen to what the Lord may be saying to you. The Lord can speak to you in many ways. He gives dreams, visions, a strong feeling, inner peace, a still voice, His word or He may even use a third party. For me in most cases, God would show me a vision or an image that would signify His direction for me and even others. This would almost always happen during prayer. Other times it is a still small voice or a strong feeling.

At first I did not recognize His voice, my strong feelings, or the images that He was showing me. As a matter of fact, initially I thought it was my imagination. As I continued to pray, His voice became clearer. I also recognized that strong tugging meant He wanted me to do something. The images also began to make more sense. As I followed the directions He has given me, everything started to fall into place. As a matter of fact, this very book was compiled due to the directions that were given in prayer. From the outline, to the writing process, it was all birthed in prayer. If I had never prayed, I would not have gotten the direction for this book and so many other ventures the Lord has led me into.

As the Lord speaks, He does not stop with direction, but He begins to give you glimpses of His will for your life. He may tell you that His will is for you to teach His word, pray for people, host seminars, write books, build a house, and so much more. The more you pray, the more He will reveal. With this constant revelation, you will develop expectations based on these words which were spoken to you in prayer. Once the Lord has spoken, your faith will be increased because if it is His will, He will make a way to bring it to pass.

> *My sheep listen to my voice; I know them, and they follow me.*
>
> *–John 10:27(NIV)*

Prayer Brings Confidence and Security

There is confidence and security in prayer. As the Lord speaks to you and becomes specific, you will have more confidence in Him. As He gives one instruction and you obey it, you will see the benefits in that instruction and that it was indeed for your good. This will cause you to have more confidence in the next instruction. You will feel secure in the decisions that you are making. Little by little your faith will begin to grow.

Even when the Lords instructions seem illogical, you will have faith that it will all work out for good and to bring Him glory. Initially, when the Lord instructed me to write this book, I felt that it was illogical. Here I am, a small island girl with absolutely no following, writing a book. As I prayed, the Lord continued to speak to me and told me to go ahead and write.

On days when I procrastinated, the Lord kept pushing me to write. It even got to the point that while in prayer, He gave me a deadline of completion. There were days when I was losing confidence and became insecure but as I prayed, He kept reminding me of His promise. If I did not have a prayer life, I would not have the confidence to complete and publish this book. I needed a constant push which the Lord kept providing in prayer.

> *Therefore I tell you, whatever you ask for in prayer, believe that you have received it, and it will be yours.*
>
> *—Mark 11:24 (NIV)*

The Vehicle of Faith

Earlier I stated how I wanted results without actually having faith but what I did not understand was faith is the vehicle to results, while prayer is the gas that fuels that vehicle (faith). Interestingly, this is displayed so much in the life and ministry of Jesus. It is often highlighted the way Jesus healed so many persons and there are some amazing stories because let's face it, Jesus is THE GREATEST! But a common denominator is the faith of the person that was healed.

The woman with the issues of blood is a great example of this.

> *And a woman was there who had been subject to bleeding for twelve years, but no one could heal her. 44 She*

*came up behind him and touched the edge of his cloak, and immediately her bleeding stopped. "Who touched me?" Jesus asked. When they all denied it, Peter said, "Master, the people are crowding and pressing against you."But Jesus said, "Someone touched me; I know that power has gone out from me. "Then the woman, seeing that she could not go unnoticed, came trembling and fell at his feet. In the presence of all the people, she told why she had touched him and how she had been instantly healed. Then he said to her, "Daughter, **your faith has healed you**. Go in peace."*

−Luke 8: 43-48(NIV)

This woman received her results because she used her faith to press through. Jesus did not tell her, "I have healed you" but He told her "Your faith has healed you". There were so many people pressing against Jesus, but yet this specific woman's touch instantly led to her healing. So much that Jesus knew that power had left Him. The difference with this woman and everyone else that was pressing against Jesus is that she had faith. She came there with the confidence that she would receive that which she had hoped for even though logically it made no sense.

Reactions and Results

Your reaction to Gods will and promises determines your results. Are your reactions ones of faith (thanking God, trusting God, comfortably resting in God) or are they ones of doubt (worrying, complaining, and impatience). Let's use a short example of a parent and child.

A father promises to purchase a jeep for his 16 year old provided that she gets her permit/license. The 16 year old does just that and we know that it is this fathers will that the child drives because let's face it, the child NEEDS transportation. We also know that it's the fathers will because he promised her he would do it, granted that she meets the requirements. Let's say the father decides to test how much the child trusts his words (promise) to get the jeep. The father wants to know if the daughter really believes him when he speaks, so he decides to wait a little while longer before he actually purchased the jeep.

At first the daughter is fine because she knows the jeep is coming. Time has passed and eventually impatience begins to kick in. The daughter begins to complain everyday saying, "dad, I'm tired", "dad, where is my jeep", "dad don't you know I need to get around?" From complaining, the daughter begins questioning her dads' ability to give her the jeep. Expressions of doubt come in. "Well maybe dad does not want me to have a jeep" "Maybe he can't afford a jeep" and so on. The daughter is now worrying and stressed, while the dad is just observing her reactions.

Here is a better version to the story. In her waiting period, the daughter says, "Dad I thank you in advance for the jeep.", "I know you will supply my need of a jeep" "I know that you love me and will always take care of me." In both scenarios, the father is still observing.

Now let's put ourselves in the shoes of the father. Which expressions would you respond to? The expressions of doubt or the expressions of faith? Similarly, this is the relationship we have with God and His promises. Our faith determines our release. It can literally determine the release date of our results.

> *And without faith it is impossible to please God, because anyone who comes to him must believe that he exists and that he rewards those who earnestly seek him.*
> *–Hebrews 11:6 (NIV)*

Ask yourself, are you feeding your faith or are you feeding doubt? Your doubt can leave you in a place of waiting longer than expected. So instead of saying, "I'm 25, now what?" you will be saying "I'm 45, now what?"

Aside from prayer, faith declarations will help in your unbelief. Once you have believed and confirmed that your desires are in alignment with God's desires, write each down. Make these declarations daily.

Now say, "Lord I thank you for_____."

Do this each morning until it is said so often it becomes natural. Be consistent and you will soon discover you believe the words. Now to be honest, Satan will try to do everything to diminish your faith because he recognizes its power. His goal is to intensify the situation so that you can focus on what you see. God told you, you would be debt free, but he reminds you that you have no money. God told you, you would have your own business, but he reminds you, you have no resources. My friend, this is when you need faith the most. This is when your prayer life must intensify and you continue to declare.

> *For we walk by faith and not by sight.*
> *–2 Corinthians 5:7(KJV)*

You must move forward by faith and not by what you see. Whether or not what is in front of you looks the way you think it should, YOU MUST WALK ANYWAY. Your results depend on it. Instead of stopping the vehicle (faith), insert more gas (prayer) until you arrive at your destination (results).

Chapter 7 Checklist

☐ Faith is relying on Gods discretion, desiring with expectation of attainment, and security in what we cannot see

☐ Your faith requires trusting God and trust is developed through prayer

☐ Prayer bring intimacy, directions, expectations, confidence, and security

☐ Faith is the vehicle to results

☐ Make daily declarations of faith

CHAPTER 8

God's Love

Thinking Out Loud...

When I think of God's love, I think of the moment I encountered His love for the first time in my life. I was around 19 years old and had just experienced a tough break up. I was heartbroken and the world as I knew it was shattered. I just remember feeling broken in more ways than I thought imaginable While in so much emotional pain and turmoil, I was trying to cope the best way I knew how, which was going to the club. I am so glad the Lord had other plans for my night. A friend of mine that was recently saved invited me to a prophetic prayer meeting. To be honest, I had absolutely no interest in attending. As a matter of fact, I had not been to church in quite some time, but my friend raved about the accurate insight that this prophetess had given into her life. I then thought I would go just to hear what would be said to me. I mean it sounded fun enough and frankly I needed some type of answers. I also figured once I am done, I will just go back to business as usual and get ready for the typical party night. Unfortunately, the prayer meeting was cancelled that night but my friend insisted we all still hang out. My friends and I decided to stop by another friend's house, sit together, and chat about God. Eventually I was asked one question that would change my life forever. "What is stopping you from giving your life to God?" Honestly, I had no answer. I mean I had what felt like a million thoughts, but one plausible answer could not escape my lips. I kept thinking, "I do not have a relationship, I feel completely abandoned. What's left?" But still no words. In that silence, I gave my life to Jesus and immediately His love came in. I could not describe it but day by day, my heart mended. Love healed me from the inside out. Till this day, my heart is completely full when I think about the love of God. I could never have enough pages to describe it or how He has displayed His love for me, but I will always remember the first time I encountered it.

from the moment you came into this world, you were constantly being taught about love. When your mother cradled you into her arms for the first time, that was love. When your father changed your poopy diapers, that was love. When your siblings asked you to play outside with them, that was love. When your aunts, uncles, and grandparents argued over who gets to keep you this weekend or whose baby you are, that was love. When you watched television and saw the happily ever after stories, that was love. Your entire life you were being trained and you learned what love looked like. While these sentiments are absolutely beautiful, they are all limited because love is seen from a limited perspective. This is the earthly perspective.

As young adults, it so important to understand the nature of God's love before you can ever accept any other love in your life. It would be difficult to move forward into the next quarter of your life if you do not know the true meaning of love.

Earthly Perspective vs. Biblical Perspective

One of the very first things you are taught about love is that love is uncontrollable. Ever wonder why you would say, 'I am FALLING in love.' You are basically saying that you cannot control who you love any more than you can control falling down. The human heart was originally associated with love because of the uncontrollable heart racing that a human feels when in the presence of someone that the person perceives to be in love with. Till this day, a heart still represents love. While this uncontrollable theory can hold some truth, there is a misconception that is associated with it. This misconception has led many persons to believe because they cannot control the feeling of falling in love; they cannot control the actions of love. In other words, earths perspective tells you, because you cannot help the fact that you love someone, you must always act on this feeling of love. It is uncontrollable, after all.

It does not matter how healthy or unhealthy the situations is, you do not have any control over your actions because you do not have control over the love you feel. This misconception gives you the license to act in ways that are irrational and just plain wrong, all in the name of love. It tells you, you can have sex with a person before marriage because you love them. You can excuse their actions because you love them. After all, you cannot help who you love, right? Wrong! While the feeling of love may feel uncontrollable at times, your actions are not synonymous with feelings. There may be times that you think you cannot control your feelings, but you can control your reaction to those feelings. You do not serve your feelings, you serve Jesus Christ

Another perspective that is taught is love is limited. This earthly perspective of love tells us that we must love with limitations and constraints. It says, you must love a person only until that person hurts you. You should love a person because you are benefitting from that love. You should love a person because the relationship is convenient. You should only love people that you actually like. So what happens when your friend says something that hurts your feelings? What happens when your spouse loses a job and can no longer support you financially? What happens when that relationship becomes inconvenient? What happens when you do not like a person? When you place limits on love, you are actually placing limits on yourself and the connections in your life. Indirectly, you are telling God that you will only love within certain constraints. Any other choice outside of those constraints will not work for you, because you know what is best for yourself based on your limited perspective. God may have the ideal spouse for you that has everything you ever wanted, however he or she may still be in the process of building financially. The limitations you have placed on yourself maybe telling you that your spouse has to have it all financially. Do you tell God no because of the limits you have placed on love?

The word of God gives us a different perspective on love that is completely refreshing.

> *The second is equally important: 'Love thy neighbor as yourself.' No other commandment is greater than these.*
> *–Mark 12:31(NIV)*

Jesus commands us to love our neighbors (everyone we come into contact with), the way that we love ourselves. This signifies that we have power over whom or what we chose to love. I cannot command someone to do something unless I knew they had control over the ability to do it. While this command shows that we have power to love (or not), we are still commanded to make the right choice. Since we are commanded to love from God himself, we no longer have the authority in selecting who to love. We are ordered to love everyone with a Godly love.

> But I tell you, love your enemies and pray for those who persecute you,
>
> —Matthew 5:44(NIV)

Not only are we commanded to love our neighbors, but we are also told to love our enemies. This severely goes against any earthly perspective we are taught. This removes the limits we have been taught to place on love. Whether that person likes or dislikes you, whether that person treats you well or not, whether that person spreads rumors about you or not, God tells us to love them. Love is meant to be limitless and not held within constraints or stipulations.

What Is Love?

We now know that the fundamental principles we have been taught about love is all wrong. A major plan of the enemy on this generation in particular is to make us feel like love is over rated. The perception is that you are to be cold hearted and only worry about self, no matter who gets hurt in the process. The message of "no love" is on television, in music, social media, and everywhere else you can think of.

God is love and love is God. He is the author and creator of it. You are made in the image of God (love), therefore when we lose love, we essentially lose God. You lose a major part of whom you are and why you exist. If you do not know God, you cannot know love because they are one in the same.

> *Whoever does not love does not know God, because God is love.*
>
> *−1 John 4:8 (NIV)*

Whenever you try to love outside of knowing God, it will always be tainted and filthy because true pure love can only come from God.

God's Love

God's love has to be one of the most indescribable experiences. Generally speaking, even human driven love is hard to explain. Love makes us irrational. Have you ever observed two persons that are truly in love? Whether it is a romantic relationship, paternal/ maternal relationship, or platonic relationship. All parties involved become protective of each other instinctually. They become concerned about the individuals well-being. Suddenly that person's health and well-being becomes more important than self. Not only that, persons act in ways that they may not usually act in order to preserve that love. This "love" becomes so precious and fragile that any threat of losing it is unthinkable. Remember we are made in the image of God.

> *So God created mankind in his own image, in the image of God he created them; male and female he created them.*
>
> *−Genesis 1:27(NIV)*

Although the love and the feelings we exude will mimic Gods love, the intensity of God's love, however cannot be matched on any level. God's love is much deeper and purer. Clear your mind. Make it a blank canvas and release all emotions. I want to as closely as I can describe Gods love for you.

Sacrificial

The first obvious picture is that God was willing to send His only Son, the one he loved so dearly to die so that He can spend eternity with you. Let that sink in. Envision sacrificing your most loved person (mother, sister, child, aunt, or husband) in order to spend eternity with someone. You did this knowing that some would still not accept you, some would curse your name, and some would rather die without giving it a second thought. In all my years, I have never met a human so willing to die for me.

> *For God so loved the world that he gave his one and only Son, that whoever believes in him shall not perish but have eternal life.*
>
> *–John 3:16(KJV)*

Long-Suffering

It does not stop there. Even when you act completely contrary, the Lord still protects those He loves. Have you ever done something so wild, so crazy, but somehow you left the situation unscratched? That was God's grace and HIS

LOVE. During my partying phase, my sister and I did a lot of wild stuff. One of the crazy things we would do continually is hitchhike with random persons. It was not luck that kept us safe from rape or being murdered, but grace and love. Imagine loving a disobedient child enough to protect them when they clearly do not deserve it? Now that's love!

> *The Lord is not slow in keeping his promise, as some understand slowness. Instead he is patient with you, not wanting anyone to perish, but everyone to come to repentance.*
>
> *−2 Peter 3:9(NIV)*

Protective

Not only is God's love sacrificial and long-suffering, it also puts our well-being first. One of the biggest hindrances' that God protects us from is ourselves. Often times, we are our biggest enemies. God loves us so much that he will remove our very habits that are hindering our progression in life. Even if we love these habits more than we love Him. Before I allowed the Lords love to come in, I had no sense of purpose. Never in a million years did I ever imagine I would be doing any of the things I am doing now. As a matter of fact, I would not have even attempted. When I allowed Gods love in my life and allowed him to guide me, he saved me from myself. The Lord will not just save you from yourself, but He will even remove any individual in your life that threatens you from truly accepting His love.

Do you think that last relationship just ended? Or maybe you accidently lost that job? No! It was the Lord stripping you to get your attention. Anything that is placed before God in your life becomes an idol. He will not allow anything to be placed before Him. God loves you so much and completely wants you to himself. He is indeed a jealous God.

> Do not worship any other god, for the Lord, whose name is Jealous, is a jealous God.
>
> –Exodus 34:14(NIV)

Prior to accepting Gods love fully, I have never experienced being loved in that manner in any form in my life. Yes, my momma loves me, yes my husband loves me, yes my sisters loves me, yes my brother loves me, yes my daddy loves me, but there is something so pure and intense about Gods love that it cannot be even placed in the same category. Even the description above does it no justice. It cannot explain how deep the love of God is. As a matter of fact, the Lord loves you so much that you did not receive this book by accident. He wants you to completely accept his love so that he can completely blow your mind.

The Effects of God's Love

TRANSFORMING

i have never met a person that has truly encountered Gods love and remained the same. God's love completely transforms. The presence of this love can shape you into who you were always meant to be. The more you accept it and engulf yourself in it, the more you will change. This is done through the renewal of your mindset. Your thoughts and perceptions will no longer be the same when you have accepted the love of God. The music that used to sound so good will become appalling. The movies that you used to watch will be uncomfortable. The curse words you used to say will sound like a dagger in your soul when uttered. Your friends will seem so lost and conversations will almost sound like you are speaking two different languages. The music, movies, words, or friends did not change. You did!

The transformation placed you in a position for God to truly mold you and develop you. When a pencil is not sharpened, it cannot operate in its purpose. The pencil has not yet undergone the change that is necessary in order to do so. When the pencil is being sharpened, layers are being peeled back all the way until it gets to the center. The pencils make up and shape is being altered. I'm sure if a pencil could feel, the removal of those layers would be painful and uncomfortable. But when the pencil is sharpened, it can now do what it was always intended to do. The pain and discomfort was necessary. It is in this way Gods love transforms us. While His love is beautiful, it transforms.

Paul, in my opinion, is one of the greatest stories of transformation. Paul was previously known as Saul and persecuted Christians. On the road to Damascus, Jesus spoke to Saul and blinded him. Now the men with Saul left Him in Damascus and he was blind for 3 days. Saul prayed to the Lord and was given a vision of a man named Ananias laying hands on him and restoring his sight. The Lord also spoke to Ananias instructing him to do just as the vision had shown, however Ananias was afraid. He did not want to be persecuted by Saul. God told Ananias to go because Saul was His chosen vessel to take the message of God to the Gentiles. Ananias did as the Lord asked and Saul regained his sight. Saul stayed with some believers and within days he was preaching the message of God.

We can see that the Lord loved Saul enough to take him off of a destructive path. The reality was Saul was on his way to hell. God took extreme measures by blinding him and literally stopping him in his tracks. But this was done in order to save Saul from himself. When Ananias did not want to heal Saul, God defended him by saying Saul was His choice. God loved him so much that despite Saul persecuting God's children, he was still Gods choice. Saul went from persecuting Christians to becoming one and preaching within a few days. What a transformation!

TRANSCENDING

when we accept Gods love, it takes us higher. Not just spiritually but in every area of our lives. When deeply wrapped in His love, there is a feeling of being uplifted that is difficult to explain. His love takes the limits off. We know this because there is a promise that comes with the love of God. This promise is that you can do all things through Christ who strengthens you. This promise alone removes the limitations from your life. You can now be confident that you can do anything in accordance to the will of God. You can be the first to own a home in your family. You can be the first to be saved. You can be the first to open a business. You can be the first to own property. You can be the first to have children in wedlock. You can do it all!

Remember God is also THE King; therefore it is not in His nature to deliver small. When you accept His love, He will give you big goals, big dreams, big thoughts, and the ability to achieve all of the above through Him. He will exceed every expectation you have ever had because that is what His love does. It transcends!

On the day of Pentecost, the believers were gathered together in one place. There was a wind and tongues of fire sat on every individual present. They were all filled with the Holy Spirit and began speaking in unknown tongues. The believers even spoke languages that they never learned. There was a transcending taking place. The believers were being taken to another level. God loved them so much that when His Son Jesus left, He sent a guide and comforter which is the Holy Spirit. This was just the beginning of Gods elevation for their lives. His love always transcends.

TRANQUILIZING

the love of God has a tranquilizing effect. It calms our mind and puts us in a peaceful state. I feel the love of God most when I am in intimate worship with Him. The feeling of His love instantly makes everything else feel small. My heart becomes so full and sometimes I cry without reason. The feeling is just so overwhelming. There is an inner peace. The amazing thing is that this feeling does not go away after worship but as you continually surround yourself with His love; it becomes a part of you. That tranquil feeling will dwell in you so you will find that you may not get angry as easily. You won't get frustrated as easily. You won't begin to worry as easily. It provides a peace that is difficult to describe but even more difficult to deny.

> *Be anxious for nothing, but in everything by prayer and supplication, with thanksgiving, let your requests be made known to God; and the peace of God, which surpasses all understanding, will guard your hearts and minds through Christ Jesus*
>
> *–Philippians 4:6-7 (NKJV)*

How to Accept God's Love

It is great that you now know all about Gods love but what good would it be if you do not know how to accept it. For some it's quite natural to accept the love of God, but for others it does not come as naturally.

1. You have to fully embrace the fact that Gods love is unconditional. There is nothing you can do that can ever separate you from Gods love. It does not matter how many mistakes you have made, God will always love you. When you go wrong, He will correct you but still love you. His love cannot be earned. There is nothing you can do to make Him love you. The love cannot be given or taken away based on human measure. Therefore it must be accepted the way that it is because nothing can be done about it.

2. Not only are you to receive Gods love, but you are to love God in return. When you truly love God, there is a beautiful connection and exchange that

takes place. When you love someone, you will do your best to make that person happy. You will not participate in actions that you know would grieve their heart. You will long to spend time with them. You will constantly have that person on your mind. You will become selfless and love that person more than yourself. Love will drive your actions. You ought to love God more than you love yourself. So much that you will literally kill your flesh daily. As you do this, it will be easier to love everyone else. Love is so filling that it spills over. It will pour from the inside out. It cannot be easily removed once it has entered your heart.

3. Learning to give and receive, just like anything else, is a process. Understand that practice makes perfect. There are times you may not feel loved, but as you go through that process, you will learn to trust the facts and not the feelings. Other times you may not have shown God love by spending time with him as frequently. Remember you are reconditioning your whole mindset to control your feelings and love the unlovable. It's a process, and not only does practice make perfect, but the Lord makes perfect. Remember God's love is unconditional so there is no limit to how many times you can practice giving and receiving it for as long as you live.

The perfect guide to love is 1 Corinthians 13. Here is a quick chart on how this chapter describes what does and does not look like love.

Love is...	Love is not...
Patient	Jealous
Kind	Boastful
Hopeful	Proud
Enduring	Rude
Rejoicing in truth	Demanding its own way
Never giving up	Irritable
Never losing faith	Rejoicing in injustice
	Keeping record of wrongdoing

This chart is not a replacement for reading the chapter since the entire chapter emphasizes the importance of love. When we finally accept Gods love and the effects have taken place in our life, we are now ready for love in other areas of our lives.

Testimony Corner

God's love for mankind goes deep...

When I became the legal age, 18, I fell in love with the world. I fell in love with my liberty to indulge in whatever my flesh desired, without conviction. Through my lens of perception, I was "okay"; I graduated high school, went straight to college, and worked part-time. I was "okay"; morally sound, honest, and a hard worker. I was "okay"; I never got in trouble with the law, nor did I do things the law prohibited, like smoke marijuana and/or drink and drive...I was "okay". I was deeply in love with the world while creating enmity with God. But, yet, His love never changed for me. Even when I walked out on Him, for a few years–committed whole heartedly to sin, He never stopped loving me. So when I returned to Him, broken, abused, dirty and defeated, God was there to embrace me. He took my hand the day I made up my mind I was coming back home. I remember one day asking God, "Is it really possible to FEEL your love?", I told Him I wanted to experience His love in a tangible way. I needed Him to be real to me because honestly, I wasn't prepared to serve someone I couldn't experience. I wasn't prepared to pretend either. I wanted to have a testimony of His love the way other believers talked about Him. Well, before

I knew it I was deeply in love with Him. And I knew He loved me back. I recall driving to the airport one day, no one else was in the car, I literally felt God's love so strong. I felt like a child who was well taken care of by her father and it felt great.

–Dayvan-Rebecca Carey

Chapter 8 Checklist

☐ Observe the difference between earths perspective and Biblical perspective

☐ Know that God is love

☐ Understand Gods love is sacrificial, long-suffering, and protective

☐ The effects of God's love is transforming, transcending, and tranquilizing

☐ Tips for accepting Gods love

CHAPTER 9

Finding Yourself

Thinking Out Loud...

When I was in the third grade, I made several mini story books. I had no idea why I did it, but I just would spend lunch breaks and free time creating stories, drawing pictures, and writing. My teacher recognized it since I would constantly bring her my story books that I made. Eventually she called my mother in and told my mother that I would make great books someday. Of course as I grew up, I wrote less and less because I became distracted with everything else this world had to offer. I loved sin and indulging in it took up so much time. When the Holy Spirit began to guide me, I found that I was often led to write. I did not see the connection right away, but I began to write daily on social media or when studying the Word. Soon I realized that I would write all the time and it just became a huge part of my life. I would literally spend hours just reading and writing without realizing or feeling the time passing me by. I no longer spent so much time partaking in worldly pleasure so I now had the opportunity to truly get to know myself. I got to understand who I am as a person and what I truly loved to do. I was finding myself.

If someone were to ask you who are you, how would you answer that? Not what you like to do, but who are you? Not what is your career title, but who are you? What if they got more specific and said to sum it up in one sentence? What would your answer be? Would you be able to answer within a few seconds, or would you have to think about it?

Knowing who you are at the age of 25 is so crucial. How can you move forward in your journey without first understanding yourself? As a matter of fact, you will benefit or lose based on the way you perceive your identity today. The one person you are sure you will have to live with for the rest of your life is YOU. Everyone else may not be present for your entire life, but you will be front row and center to every chapter of your life.

Therefore there is no need to emphasize how important it is to know who you are. We have talked about the past, voids, and fear and they all have one thing in common. The ability to steal your identity. The past will tell you that you are what you have experienced. The void will tell you that you are empty and the way you fill that emptiness is who you are. Fear will tell you whatever situation you are in now, is who you are, therefore there is no moving forward.

Once your identity is stolen, then anyone can dictate who you are, whether it is true or not. How dangerous is that?

Background Check

There is a saying that says, "In order to know who you are, you have to know where you come from." Now chances are you know who is your mother and father, but do you really know where you come from? Let us do a background check to the creation of the first man and woman.

> *Then God said, "Let us make human beings in our image, to be like us. They will reign over the fish in the sea, the birds in the sky, the livestock, all the wild animals on the earth, and the small animals that scurry along the ground." So God created human beings in his own image. In the image of God he created them; male and female he created them. Then God blessed them and said, "Be fruitful and multiply. Fill the earth and govern it. Reign over the fish in the sea, the birds in the sky, and the animals that scurry along the ground."*
>
> *–Genesis 1: 26-28 (NLT)*

You are created by God. Know that the God of the universe made you. He chose your hair color, your skin, your eyes, and your mouth. Every detail of your life, from who your parents are to your gifts and talents were all perfectly orchestrated by Him. In other words, He created your identity. There was no mistake. You were not just the lucky sperm that made it to the egg. You were carefully and thoughtfully planned out by God Himself. You are the creation of the King.

Being the creation of the King, it only makes sense that He would create you to reign. In the garden, the Lord gave Adam the responsibility to rule the earth and everything that the earth contained. This shows you were meant to rule and rulers are leaders of the world. It should not be the other way around. Other than God, there is nothing else that should rule or control you. Not friends, not your habits, not your thoughts, and certainly not your feelings. Anything that tries to rule you, is seeking to steal your identity. Be careful. By stealing your identity, these "rulers" are trying to replace the true ruler in your life, which is God.

You are made in the image of God. An image is another word for reflection. Therefore you are like God. You hold characteristics and similarities to God. You were not made to bare a resemblance to some random person but to the all-powerful God. Take a moment to reflect on that!

Think about it. You are your mother and fathers child, therefore you look like them in one way or another, perhaps walk like them, maybe even sound like them. It's the same thing with God. We feel love, anger, compassion, desires, and grief, which are all characteristics of God. I find that there are so many persons that miss the close connection and tie that we as humans have to God. It is often forgotten that we came from Him and so we have so many similarities to who He is.

You were meant to be fruitful and reproduce. To be fruitful is just another way to say to bring forth fruit. When a person speaks of reproduction, it is always thought of in the physical sense; however there are many ways of reproduction. How does one bring forth fruit? Whenever I think of baring fruit, a plant or tree comes to mind. Every plant that was created has seed which is necessary to re-plant, produce fruit, and new trees.

From creation, this seed (as little as it may be) has everything it needs in order to become a tree and produce fruit. Growth with the seed, however, does not just happen. It comes through the planting, watering, and nurturing of the seed. When God instructs us to be fruitful, it is because the seed of reproduction or multiplication is already placed on the inside of us. When reproduction takes place, there are others created in the likeness of the original creation. An apple seed makes apples and cannot produce a fruit outside of an apple (its likeness). Therefore when God tells us to reproduce, we are to plant our seed, which is our gifting (natural and spiritual). Water it, through the living water of the Holy Spirit. And nurture it, which is using it, protecting it, and mastering it. Then we will see fruit which is other believers being brought forth. You were born to be a reproducer.

Identification Card: Jesus Christ

If you were created by The King, created to rule, created with the characteristics of The King, and created to reproduce other rulers, then that can only mean that you are created to be royal. When you see a queen, you just know that she is a queen. She does not have to make an announcement and say, "Hey everybody! I'm a queen!" You can tell by her walk, the way her head is held high, her attire, her speech, and everything else just screams queen.

This is because from birth, she was trained to first of all, know who she is and secondly, to act in accordance with this identity. If this queen was never told she was a queen and trained, she would not know how to act like royalty.

Although you were created to be royalty, sin disconnects the relationship between God and man. While God loves you, He hates sin. We are all born in sin, therefore from birth there is a disconnection. As long as sin is ruling your life, there is a severing of ties. This connection is regained through Jesus Christ. When you accept Jesus as your Lord and Savior, and are reborn, then you are now adopted into the family of God. You moved from being a creation of God to being a child of God. You are royalty.

> *Jesus replied, "I tell you the truth, unless you are born again, you cannot see the Kingdom of God."*
>
> *—John 3:3 (NLT)*

A major step to finding yourself is rooting your identity in Jesus Christ. You will never find your true self until you accept Jesus Christ as your Lord and Savior. You will need to be reconciled to your Heavenly Father in order to obtain your royal identity. It does not matter what you did the night before you accepted your royal lineage, your identity has now been restored to its intended original state. You must be confident in who you are, because there are so many things in this world seeking to steal this identity. You are royalty! This always reminds me of Jesus and his disciples. In order to find themselves, they had to let go of who they thought they were.

As Jesus was walking along, he saw a man named Matthew sitting at his tax collector's booth.

"Follow me and be my disciple," Jesus said to him. So Matthew got up and followed Him.

–Matthew 9:9 (NLT)

Matthew clearly identified with being a tax collector. However when Jesus called him, he did not hesitate, but he left his old identity behind. He chose to step into his new lineage of royalty. The identity that God intended for him. If Matthew did not take this step, would we be reading about him today? Your future in royalty is so much better than your past. Follow Him and find yourself.

Training

Once you are reconciled back to your royal lineage, there is some training that must take place. The trainer is none other than the Holy Spirit. The Holy Spirit is there to guide you and develop you in this new found identity. When you are acting contrary to the ways of the King, he will prick your heart and remind you that you should no longer act in this way. He will not let you slip back into the old lifestyle without warning. Some people may refer to it as a conscious, but it is actually the Holy Spirit. While no one is perfect, when the trainer is speaking, it is important to listen. If you chose to ignore the Holy Spirit, soon your heart will become hardened to His voice.

As you learn from the guidance of the Holy Spirit, He will reveal to you more and more of who you are. Because you are not cluttered by the perceived "pleasure" of sin, you get to understand what you really love and who you are. Do not be afraid to ask God questions. He created you and can answer any questions about yourself that you want to know. He can unveil and remove any doubts that you may have about your royal heritage. He may not answer the first time you ask, but as you continually seek Him, He will answer.

Am I Really Royal?

Now let's be honest. There are days you may not feel royal. Actually there are times you may feel quite the opposite. There are times you may be tempted to not even consider yourself to be a child of God. It happens! There are no exceptions to the human feelings. Even in these times, it is important that more than ever, you hold on to your identity and the word of God. It is crucial not to act outside of the Holy Spirits training. Before Jesus began His ministry, He was tempted by the devil. His second temptation was quite interesting.

> *Then the devil took him to the holy city, Jerusalem, to the highest point of the Temple, and said, "If you are the Son of God, jump off! For the Scriptures say, 'He will order his angels to protect you. And they will hold you up with their hands so you won't even hurt your foot on a stone'. Jesus responded, "The Scriptures also say, 'You must not test the Lord your God.'"*
>
> *–Matthew 4:5-7 (NLT)*

The devil asked Jesus, IF you are the Son of God. He was questioning the identity of Jesus. Satan was telling Jesus to prove himself. The issue is that anytime a person feels the need to prove anything to someone else, it is a sign of insecurity. I know that I am married to my husband. I know that I am His wife. Being secure in my marriage however is different from knowing I am married. So Satan was not just testing if Jesus knew His identity, he was testing His security in His identity.

Bare in mind, Jesus was in the wilderness fasting for 40 days and 40 nights. He was extremely hungry. I am sure He did not feel like a King. Of course He was physically weak. Despite this feeling, Jesus stayed grounded in who He was. He stood on the scriptures as His foundation during the time of testing when His feelings were vulnerable. Jesus was secure in His identity.

Here are some quick scriptures anytime you are feeling like you are in an identity crisis:

> But the person who is joined to the Lord is one spirit with him.
>
> *−1 Corinthians 6:17(NKJV)*

> But to all who believed him and accepted him, he gave the right to become children of God.
>
> *−John 1:12 (NLT)*

> God decided in advance to adopt us into his own family by bringing us to himself through Jesus Christ. This is what He wanted to do, and it gave Him great pleasure
>
> *−Ephesians 1:5 (NLT)*

But you are not like that, for you are a chosen people. You are royal priests, a holy nation, God's very own possession. As a result, you can show others the goodness of God, for he called you out of the darkness into his wonderful light.

—1 Peter 2:9 (NLT)

See how very much our Father loves us, for he calls us his children, and that is what we are! But the people who belong to this world don't recognize that we are God's children because they don't know him.

—1 John 3:1(NLT)

Testimony Corner

In a world filled with so many thoughts and ideas about humankind, it's not difficult to see how one can be confused or perplexed about his/her identity and purpose. Challenging thoughts of whether the Almighty God exists; if His Word is true; and His role in an individual's life bombards the mind and the airways. But thank God for His mercy!

Though we may never have all the answers, my search for true identity, purpose and confidence has ended in the place of prayer. Prayer has been the catalyst for the discovery of the aforementioned vital ingredients of a person's life.

Great levels of exposure, intimacy and exchange have occurred and made the world of difference, all in the place of prayer. Of course there will be obstacles and times of discouragement but I'm reminded of the fact that God rewards those who purpose and move to seek Him diligently. Will you become a diligent seeker? The only way to find the calm to the storm of your identity search is to lose yourself in prayer. I've found the courage, boldness and the answers to the pathway to follow because I was fortunate to taste of His goodness

The choice is yours…what will your testimony be? Selah!

–Lynden Seymour

Chapter 9 Checklist

- ☐ Know your background and lineage

- ☐ Accept your royal heritage through Christ Jesus

- ☐ Allow the Holy Spirit to train you

- ☐ Be secure and grounded in your identity in Christ through scriptures

CHAPTER 10

Purpose

Thinking Out Loud...

When I gave my life to the Lord, my next questions was now what? For such a long time, being saved was the destination. Now that I arrived at the destination, I needed clarity on what was next. So I prayed and asked God daily. I mean literally, like a nagging child, I asked Him morning, noon, and night. I seriously thought the first day I asked, He would send some big sign or maybe an angelic messenger but that never worked out. The Lord answered me in one of the most unexpected ways. He spoke to me through my desires. The Lord awakened the desire for reading, writing, and praying. In addition to this, the Lord also awakened a fire to share his gospel with others. These desires were so heavy, strong, and unquenchable that I just could not contain it. The more I wrote, read, prayed, and shared, the more I wanted to do it. Opinions no longer mattered, time did not matter, and nothing else mattered. I felt it with so much passion and love that I just knew, this is what I was born to do.

Why am I here? What was I created for? What am I born to do? What is my purpose? Do I even have one? These questions are the hardest questions any person will ever have to ask themselves. Discovering the answer feels even harder. In the quiet solitude, these are the reigning questions persons undergoing the Quarter-Life Crisis ask themselves.

What Is Purpose?

Purpose is simply the reason God created a person. When you thinks of purpose, you usually think of some complicated elaborate design. However this may not always be the case. Think of a newborn baby that only lived a few days. As painful and heart-wrenching that experience is, that child's life served a purpose. Perhaps that beautiful life brought the parents closer together or strengthened the testimonies of all those affected. Although we may not understand, know that the good, bad, and everything in between works according to Gods plan or purpose.

Furthermore, because we are united with Christ, we have received an inheritance from God, for he chose us in advance, and he makes everything work according to his plan.

—Ephesians 1:11 (NLT)

It does not matter how big or small you perceive a purpose to be, but it is all according to the Will of God. What is considered small in the eyes of man may be big in Gods eyesight.

Purpose Comes Through Jesus Christ

While I cannot specifically answer how your whole life's purpose will unfold, I can tell you that your purpose will not be outside of Jesus Christ. When God created you, He did not create you with the intention of serving yourself, but you were created to serve Him.

That's the whole story. Here now is my final conclusion: Fear God and obey his commands, for this is everyone's duty. God will judge us for everything we do, including every secret thing, whether good or bad.

—Ecclesiastes 12: 13-14 (NLT)

The enemy has a plan for those who are willing to follow him, which is the road to destruction. The Lord, however, has a purpose for His children. Plans can be changed, but a purpose is fixed from birth. When you become a believer, you no longer operate in plans, but you begin to operate in purpose. This purpose is to bring honor and glory to God so that others may come to know Him. This is why purpose can only come through Jesus Christ.

> *Therefore go and make disciples of all nations, baptizing them in the name of the Father and the Son and the Holy Spirit.*
>
> *–Matthew 28:19 (NIV)*

There however, are many paths and expressions to fulfilling this ultimate purpose. You can call them assignments which all leads to Gods ultimate purpose of bringing Him glory. Feeding a neighbor, helping those in need, loving each other are just a few of the ways to bringing persons into the kingdom of God and fulfilling this ultimate purpose.

Importance of Purpose

There are some that may find the topic of purpose cliché; however purpose is so important to the life of a believer. One of the main attributes of purpose is it will keep you going. There are some mornings that purpose will wake you up. You may not feel like getting up, you may be in a slump, you may just not be in the best mood. But knowing that you have a purpose to fulfill will give you the boost you need to get up and do what you know you were meant to do. Purpose will also bring accountability between you and God. When you decide to be obedient to God and operate in your purpose, you know He will hold you accountable for not acting in accordance with what you know He has required of you. This accountability will aid you in the completion of purpose.

Signs of Purpose

You may be in the process of birthing your unique way of attaining Gods purpose without even realizing it. Just like a woman that is pregnant, there are signs during the pregnancy and right before the labor. The closer the woman is to giving birth, the more the signs become prevalent. The signs that the inception of purpose has been implanted in your spiritual womb are:

1. Shift in desires
2. Stripping
3. Testing
4. Awakening of gifts

One clear sign that purpose has been implanted is that your desire for knowing and understanding your purpose will increase. You begin to feel lost and wonder what is next in your life. Even though you may have an indication of what your purpose is, you now want to know more. There is a deep yearning that you just cannot seem to help. You do not feel like you can continue along the same path you have for all these years because your desires have shifted.

You will also find that what once use to excite you is just not working out anymore. The parties, the friends, the family, and so on. You feel completely over it. Instead of going out on a Saturday night, you would rather do something that will bring more fulfillment. You cannot explain it, but your old ways are just stripping away and you desire more.

The Lord is actually stripping you in order to show you that He is all that you need. Before He brings you into the fullness of your purpose, He has to remove certain habits and people from your life so that He gets all the glory and not them. Not everyone can go where you are going.

No matter who you are, you will be tested. God will test the hearts of His children. Abraham is an example of this. God asked Abraham to sacrifice his only son. This was the son that Abraham thought he could not have. This was the son of his old age that he loved dearly. God did not want Abraham to actually kill his son, but He was testing him. Before the Lord can bring you into His purpose for your life, He is ensuring that He can trust you. The testing is a sign that the birthing of purpose is near.

When you are going into purpose, there is often an awakening of both natural and spiritual gifts. The gifts that you did not know you had will begin to come forth. The gifts that you knew you had that were dormant will suddenly be bursting from the inside. You will be given new gifts. The intensity and swiftness that this happens will indicate how close you are to birthing purpose.

How Do I Find My Path to Fulfilling Purpose?

ASK GOD

as you know, we are all unique and the Lord speaks to each person differently. The Lord may not speak to everyone through their desires like me. He may audibly tell you your purpose, someone else may see a vision, or another may

I'm 25. Now What? • 193

sense it in their spirit. One thing is for certain. In order to obtain an answer to anything, a question must be asked. In order to identify your purpose, seek the Creator and be persistent in seeking. Do not expect to ask the Lord, what is my purpose today and if a reply does not come instantly, simply leave it alone. Just like me, you may have to ask for months but when the answer finally comes, it is so worth it. God is not the author of confusion therefore He will bring clarity and peace.

BE PATIENT WITH YOUR UNIQUE PATH

Understand that your path to fulfilling purpose is as unique as you are. Be patient with yourself. Everything that God creates is diverse. Look at human beings and our various shapes, complexions, and personalities. Look at the plants and the animals. The uniqueness of your purpose will bring in diverse groups of people that you are called to help. The persons that you can reach are specific to you. Do not be alarmed if your set path does not look like someone else's. Your path to purpose was created just for you.

YOUR GIFTS AND BATTLES ARE YOUR HINTS

purpose often ties in with both your gifts and your biggest battle. What are you naturally good at? Do you have an eye for design? Are you technology savvy? Are you an intellectual person? Are you a good speaker? These gifts or expressions that the Lord has given you are actually the tools that will be used to get to your purpose which is to bring glory to Him. King David was an excellent musician and warrior. It was these natural gifts that got him into the palace. These gifts were the doorways God used. They led to the people of the kingdom knowing him and loving him until eventually he became king. Now being king was not David's ultimate purpose. His ultimate purpose was to bring honor, glory, and the people of Israel to God. Being King was an assignment here on earth.

More often than not, another indication of where your path will lead is your greatest battle. The enemy knows the specific arenas God has called you to, therefore He will try to sabotage it before its inception while you are unaware. A young man may be called to be revelatory in the Word, therefore this man may have a battle with believing Gods word. The enemy will tell that person lies like the gospel of Jesus Christ is not real and was only written by men without the Holy Spirit. He is trying to abort purpose before implantation has taken place. A young woman may be called to minister about purity so the enemy will tell her that there is nothing wrong with fornication as long as you use a condom. Again, he is trying to abort purpose before implantation has taken place.

BE COMMITTED AND UNAFRAID

god creates your purpose. Therefore when you question purpose, you are actually questioning God. You are questioning Gods ability or desire to deliver on His promises, which is completely against the character of God. Being in such a fast paced society where everything is at your fingertips, it is easy to forget that some of the best things in life take time to develop and build. Your purpose will not always unfold before you as quickly as you would like, but it is not a microwave process. No matter what, you must stay committed.

There are many persons that will not understand you or the path to fulfilling Gods purpose for your life. Some will even criticize it and say that it is not God because it does not make sense to them. To be honest, sometimes it will not even make sense to you because Gods ways are not our ways. Despite their unbelief, the reality is God did not give them the purpose. He gave it to you. If he wanted their approval, He would have told them and not you. How can someone who has not purposed you dictate your path to purpose? How can you even lead yourself when you did not purpose yourself? Stand firm and remember that God called you. You must be persistent and committed.

Do not be afraid. You are not being blindly led. Your purpose is not unknown or hidden because God knows it all. He will reveal it to you but parts of it may be hidden from you for Gods glory. Sometimes the Lord does not give the whole story because He knows it may overwhelm you. You may feel like it is too much for you and abort. Trust that God will reveal it in His time when He is ready.

Spiritual Gifts

As you begin to operate in purpose, the Lord will awaken spiritual gifts within you to assist you in completing this purpose. These spiritual gifts will both bring you closer to God and be a sign to unbelievers that God is indeed real. Each person's spiritual gifts are different. Some will be able to prophesy, another may be able to heal, and another will be able to speak or interpret tongues. God decides which gifts He will give to each believer. After all He knows best.

> 'In the last days,' God says, 'I will pour out my Spirit upon all people. Your sons and daughters will prophesy. Your young men will see visions, and your old men will dream dreams. In those days I will pour out my Spirit even on my servants—men and women alike—and they will prophesy. And I will cause wonders in the heavens above and signs on the earth below— blood and fire and clouds of smoke. The sun will become dark, and the moon will turn blood red. Before that great and glorious day of the Lord arrives. But everyone who calls on the name of the Lord will be saved.'
>
> *–Acts 2:17-21 (NIV)*

As soon as you have accepted Jesus, you become filled with the Holy Spirit. None the less, all of your spiritual gifts are not awakened at this very moment. This will take deep prayer and communication with God. Consistent prayer will lead to the birthing of the spiritual gifts that the Lord has placed in you.

In some cases, God will send midwives or other believers in your life to assist in the awakening of spiritual gifts and the birthing of purpose. This was certainly the case with me. The Lord sent others that were stronger than I was spiritually to empower me. As we connected and prayed, my spiritual gifts began to awaken. God has a way

Prayer + Spiritual Gifts = Purpose

of surrounding you with men and women of God that will pray with you, hold you accountable, and encourage you to keep going.

Tips for Operating in Purpose

Procrastination is the killer of purpose. When the Lord gives instruction, it is imperative to move right away. When you procrastinate and tell God you will do it tomorrow, you are actually telling God that you know you will have tomorrow. Your life is a vapor. The harsh truth is, you do not know if you have until tomorrow. Even if Gods instruction does not make sense, move immediately because when you delay Gods instruction, you are actually delaying your purpose.

Walk in authority and be bold in what God has told you to do. God would not give you the vision if He has not yet made the provision. Even in times of doubt, continue to walk in authority because the fight is already fixed. God has already won.

This point is so big that I have to reemphasize it. Consistently seek the Lord in prayer and await His instructions. The enemies' goal is to sabotage purpose. Since prayer leads to purpose, he combats prayer in order to delay the birthing of spiritual gifts. The fight for purpose just like any other fight is not physical, but it is spiritual. Therefore you must war using your weapon of prayer.

Purpose and Eternity

What is the point of all of this purpose talk? Does it matter if I even fulfill it or not? The completion or incompletion of your purpose on earth will determine how your eternity will be spent. You read that correctly. Your obedience to fulfilling Gods purpose on earth will determine where you will go when earth is passed away. There are only two destinations, heaven or hell.

> *Not everyone who calls out to me, 'Lord! Lord!' will enter the Kingdom of Heaven. Only those who actually do the will of my Father in heaven will enter.*
>
> *–Matthew 7:21 (NIV)*

Your purpose is not dependent on earthly and material accomplishments because earth is not your home. I was so guilty of this. I felt my purpose was wrapped up in how accomplished I was. I thought if I failed at being accomplished according to the worlds standards, then I failed my purpose. This could not be further from the truth. I am so grateful that God showed me that my purpose is not for any reward on earth, but for eternity.

Here is a parable that accurately portrays the importance of walking in purpose and being obedient. There are two categories. Those that magnify what God has given them and bring people into the kingdom. Then there are those that hold on to what God has given them without using it for His glory.

"Again, the Kingdom of Heaven can be illustrated by the story of a man going on a long trip. He called together his servants and entrusted his money to them while he was gone. He gave five bags of silver to one, two bags of silver to another, and one bag of silver to the last—dividing it in proportion to their abilities. He then left on his trip.

"The servant who received the five bags of silver began to invest the money and earned five more. The servant with two bags of silver also went to work and earned two more. But the servant who received the one bag of silver dug a hole in the ground and hid the master's money.

"After a long time their master returned from his trip and called them to give an account of how they had used his money. The servant to whom he had entrusted the five bags of silver came forward with five more and said, 'Master, you gave me five bags of silver to invest, and I have earned five more.'

"The master was full of praise. 'Well done, my good and faithful servant. You have been faithful in handling this small amount, so now I will give you many more responsibilities. Let's celebrate together!'

"The servant who had received the two bags of silver came forward and said, 'Master, you gave me two bags of silver to invest, and I have earned two more.'

"The master said, 'Well done, my good and faithful servant. You have been faithful in handling this small amount, so now I will give you many more responsibilities. Let's celebrate together!'

"Then the servant with the one bag of silver came and said, 'Master, I knew you were a harsh man, harvesting crops you didn't plant and gathering crops you didn't cultivate. I was afraid I would lose your money, so I hid it in the earth. Look, here is your money back.'

"But the master replied, 'You wicked and lazy servant! If you knew I harvested crops I didn't plant and gathered crops I didn't cultivate, why didn't you deposit my money in the bank? At least I could have gotten some interest on it.'

"Then he ordered, 'Take the money from this servant, and give it to the one with the ten bags of silver. To those who use well what they are given, even more will be given, and they will have an abundance. But from those who do nothing, even what little they have will be taken away. Now throw this useless servant into outer darkness, where there will be weeping and gnashing of teeth.'

–Matthew 25:14-30 (NLT)

The silver in this parable can represent anything God has given you. Has he entrusted you with money, talent, purpose? Are you using what he has given you in order to bring other believers into the kingdom and bring multiplication? What are you doing with what He has given you? The way that you treat the things he has entrusted you with, including your purpose on earth will determine whether you hear well done my good and faithful servant or depart from me I never knew you.

Is your path to fulfilling Gods purpose a priority in your life? Or do you treat it as if you will get to it whenever you can? Do you think you are too young and you need more time? If you have answered yes, the time to truly seek God is now. It is time to begin walking in purpose. There is great urgency in what God has called you to do and you must treat it as such. This is no time to slumber and hope everything falls into place. Just like the servants that were given silver, you must work so that multiplication and duplication can take place. It makes absolutely no sense to trade a few years of relaxation and fun for an eternity of torment. Pursue your purpose with passion. Eternity is on the line!

Chapter 10 Checklist

- ☐ Understand what is Purpose

- ☐ Know the importance of purpose

- ☐ Recognize the signs of purpose

- ☐ Tips on finding the path to purpose

- ☐ Prayer births spiritual gifts

- ☐ Tips for operating in purpose

- ☐ The relationship between purpose and eternity

To contact Author Gilberta Thompson, please:

Visit us Online at:
www.gilbertathompson.com

Facebook:
Gilberta Thompson

Instagram:
Gilberta Thompson

E-mail:
hello@gilbertathompson.com

Made in the USA
Monee, IL
19 June 2023

36169321R00125